FINNTASTIC GAMES

THE FINN CLASS AT THE LONDON 2012 OLYMPIC SAILING COMPETITION

ROBERT DEAVES

Published by Robert Deaves
for the International Finn
Association

www.finnclass.org

Copyright © Robert Deaves
and the International Finn
Association, 2012

A Finn Class Publication

First Edition 2012

Some material in this book
was originally published by the
International Finn Association.

ISBN 978-0-9559001-3-6

Designed by Robert Deaves

Whilst every care was taken in
the preparation of this book
to ensure that the information
contained herein is correct,
neither the author nor the
publisher can accept any
responsibility for any errors or
inaccuracies that may remain.

CONTENTS

PREFACE
HISTORY IN THE MAKING

Top to bottom: The Finn racing was some of the closest for many years, while the medal race was one of the most watched sailing races in history • Jonas Høgh-Christensen, Ben Ainslie and Jonathan Lobert on the podium • Ben Ainslie celebrates in front of the crowd after the medal race

THE LONDON 2012 OLYMPIC SAILING COMPETITION at Weymouth & Portland was a brilliant showcase for the sport of sailing. Everything ran to perfection. The wind, the sunshine and the spectators all turned up in equally ample measures to produce a sailing extravaganza second to none.

For those who were competing and for those who just watched from the water or on shore, the event will live long in the memory as a perfect example of sporting excellence amid a fantastic competitive atmosphere

For many the Finn class provided the highlight of the regatta with Ben Ainslie's struggle to win his fourth consecutive Olympic gold medal – and fifth medal in total – to become the most successful Olympic sailor of all time, making news across the globe. With Ainslie's attempt on this record, attention on the Finn class was always going to be intense and over the course of the Olympics it is fair to say that the class attracted more media attention than any other event in Weymouth. In addition, the Finn medal race was probably the most watched sailing race in history.

EIGHT DAYS

The Finn class racing opened on Sunday 29 July with a series of 10 opening races before the deciding medal race on Sunday 5 August. Over those eight days the sailors became famous as the images and stories of their struggles against the conditions and each other emerged from the field of play out in Weymouth Bay.

This was the first sailing event ever at an Olympics that had ticketed spectators. The downside of this was that the only sailing area that could be adequately viewed from the shore was under the Nothe peninsula in an expanse of water that became famous for its shifty and fitful wind. Vast numbers of the public paid to sit on the grassy banks in the summery conditions to watch the sailing below them. Equally large numbers also sat either side of the viewing area outside the fence and got just as good a view, while tens of thousands more visited the free site on Weymouth beach with its two enormous screens relaying live images of both Olympic sailing and other sports.

THRILLING

Like most classes, the Finns started and finished on the Nothe course, while spending the rest of the regatta on the offshore courses in Weymouth Bay. As the cameras portrayed with startling clarity, the sailing and the racing on the offshore courses was a magnificent and thrilling showcase. The big waves and big winds finally showed sailing to the viewing public as a physical sport for athletes rather than as the rich man's pastime that it has so often been misconstrued to be. At long last the sport was alive and interesting.

For each of the 24 Finn sailors, a spot on the starting line at the Olympics was the culmination of at least four years' hard work. Along the way there were many trials and tribulations, triumphs and upsets for this group of elite athletes, each with his own story to tell.

JOURNEY

Ainslie himself had experienced a turbulent year as he prepared for his record-breaking attempt. During an incident at the 2011 Finn Gold Cup in Perth, where he was upset with the interference a media boat had caused during a critical race, he had famously boarded the boat and remonstrated with the camera crew. That action cost him the world title and almost cost him his place at the Olympics. Then he had to make the tough decision to undergo surgery on his back just seven months before the Games. Though still in pain, he survived all this and his brutal training programme to dominate the 2012 Finn Gold Cup in Falmouth to win his sixth Finn world title in some extreme conditions. Only he knows how deep he had to dig into his mental and physical reserves to maintain his performance and concentration through to the Olympics medal race on Sunday 5 August.

Jonas Høgh-Christensen was sailing at his third Olympics and even though he knew he had the ability to win a medal, converting that belief into a podium place was no easy task. He was a medal favourite back in 2008 but failed to perform to his and others' expectations. After that, he had taken time out and found a new career, but the need was still there and he came back stronger than ever to peak at just the right time. Nevertheless, even he must have been surprised to find himself leading the fleet from day one all the way through to the captivating medal race. It was not what anyone was expecting.

In contrast to the other two medalists, Jonathan Lobert was sailing his first Olympics. After watching one of his compatriots win the bronze in 2008 in Qingdao on the result of the medal race, he was set to repeat this feat in 2012. As a Finn sailor he was part of the new generation of athletes that the fleet had attracted in recent years. Younger, taller, stronger, fitter, he epitomised the athleticism of the class. Also he had always produced his best performances and results in Weymouth and 2012 was going to be no exception.

The stories of these three sailors are just part of the mosaic that made up the story of the 24 athletes in the Finn fleet at the 2012 Olympic Games. All were on an exceptional journey with many rewards; all their stories are told in this book.

CONTENT

Over the course of the Olympics the Finn class released a series of 21 press releases consisting of previews, interviews, race reports and wraps, all telling the sailors' stories on and off the water. There was

such a high level of content produced that it seemed like a natural progression to present it all in one place as a seamless narrative, a record of history in the making.

Those press releases form the basis of this book. While each 'chapter' has been edited and amended to provide a better style for a book rather than the immediacy required from daily press releases, a conscious effort has been made to preserve the anticipation and growing excitement that the press releases revealed as the event progressed. Therefore, later outcomes and knowledge have not been worked into prior narratives to allow the reader to discover the development of the story through the build-up, the opening series and into the medal race.

STORY

If it was a story well worth telling the first time, then it is also worth telling a second time. The story in this book will go down in history as one of the defining moments of the 2012 Olympic Games and also as one of the defining moments in the history of sailing. Only 24 sailors can say they were a part of that moment, but everyone who watched and read and experienced the power, the emotion and the excitement of the moment has an inspirational tale to tell future generations. These stories are a tribute to those 24 Finn sailors.

ONE
A BRIEF HISTORY OF THE FINN CLASS AT THE OLYMPIC GAMES

Top to bottom: Serge Maury leads the fleet in 1972 in Kiel on his way to gold • Paul Elvstrøm won his final Olympic gold medal in generally light winds in 1960 in Naples • In 1968 the Olympics were in Acapulco, again in mainly light winds, and Valentin Mankin won the gold

THE FINN MADE ITS FIRST appearance at the Olympic Games back in 1952. That year Paul Elvstrøm won the second of his four gold medals on his way to setting a record that lasted for 52 years. More than five decades later Ben Ainslie stood on the brink of breaking that record, as he has broken so many other records in his 10 years in the class. In doing so it would be one of the defining moments of the London 2012 Olympic Games.

The Finn was the oldest dinghy class used at the 2012 Olympic Games. In fact 2012 marked the class's 60th anniversary of inclusion in the Games and represented its 16th appearance. Over those 60 years it has evolved and embraced new technologies but is fundamentally the same design.

But to go back to the very beginning...

The Olympics in **1952** were assigned to **Helsinki**, Finland, and the Finnish Yachting Association – who had been assigned the job of selecting the class for the Monotype – ran a competition for a new boat designed specifically for the Olympics that could also be used for sailing competitions in Scandinavia.

The Finn was selected from a design entered by Swedish Olympian Rickard Sarby. Paul Elvstrøm swept the board to win by nearly 3,000 points from Charles Currey of Great Britain, who took silver. Elvstrøm won four of the seven races in a fleet of 28 boats and set a standard that has never been equalled. In spite of badly injuring his hand before the sixth race, Sarby just managed to win the bronze.

ELVSTRØM

Elvstrøm – who won his first gold medal at the 1948 Olympics in Torbay in the Firefly class – won because of his hiking technique, which he had developed while practising in his own boat. Most of his competitors were sitting on the sidedeck instead of hiking on the sheer guard. In addition, Elvstrøm attached a sort of traveller to his boat, which was not supplied by the organiser. Most competitors considered this alteration to be illegal, but the Dane got away with it. However, after the fifth race, when it was already certain that he had won the gold medal, Elvstrøm removed the device again, in order to calm the critics.

The Finn had proved to be such a great competitive boat in the 1952 Olympics that it was retained as the Monotype again for the **1956** Olympics in **Melbourne**, Australia. Again, Elvstrøm slaughtered the opposition, this time with five wins in his score. Going into the last race it looked as though the American John Marvin, who had never raced a Finn before, might topple the Belgian André Nelis since they were level on points. But Nelis pulled out all the stops and kept Marvin covered whilst notching up a second place himself.

For **1960** in **Naples**, Italy, there was a great increase to 35 Finns and Elvstrøm did it again. This time he won only three races and had to withdraw from the last through illness, but he was never lower than fifth in conditions that did not allow him to gain by his fantastic strength and endurance. This was the year that Russia arrived as a top sailing nation and in the Finns the silver medal was won by Alexandr Chuchelov. Nelis of Belgium took bronze.

In **Tokyo**, Japan, in **1964**, for the first time the supplied hulls were fibreglass instead of wood. Germany was the leading nation in the Finn in 1964, and Willy Kuhweide, who was selected only at the last moment and despite a severe infection of the middle ear, led the fleet into the final race. Peter Barrett and Henning Wind stayed close to each other during that race and finished seventh and 10th, allowing Kuhweide once again to take line honours and gold.

FLAWLESS

The **1968** Games were in Mexico with the sailing at **Acapulco**. Some picked Wind, who had just won the Finn Gold Cup, while others favoured Kuhweide or Jörg Bruder, the Brazilian who had won the Pan American Games. Few believed that Valentin Mankin, the veteran Russian Finn sailor and an excellent heavy weather helmsman, had much of a chance in the light weather so typical of Acapulco. But Mankin surprised everyone with a week of almost flawless tactical racing. Never below seventh at any mark, he beat Hubert Raudaschl of Austria by almost 42 points. Fabio Albarelli of Italy won the bronze.

In a venue synonymous with strong winds and heavy weather sailing, no-one was prepared for two weeks of mild weather and light winds at the **1972** Olympics in **Kiel**, Germany. Before the Olympics there was a controversy about the masts supplied by the organiser. Most of the competitors favoured the old wooden masts, which they were used to, and only a few had experience with the new aluminium masts they were forced to use. The competition ended with some big names down the scoreboard. Serge Maury of France won the gold while Elias Hatzipavlis from Greece got silver and Victor Potapov from Russia bronze. The decisive race was the fifth, when only three boats finished within the time limit.

CHANGE

There was another change for the **1976** Olympics in **Kingston**, Ontario, Canada. As usual, the organisers supplied the hulls, but for the first time the sailors were allowed to bring their own sails and masts. Not until the weather mark of the last race was it clear where the medals would go. First around was Jochen Schümann from the German Democratic Republic with a tenacious cover over Andrei Balashov of the Soviet Union. Australian John Bertrand, the other contender for the gold, was a distant 12th. Although later passed by two boats, Schümann finished

ahead of the Russian and the Australian to assure his win. As striking as Schümann's excellent performance was the poor showing of the pre-race favourites, David Howlett of England and Serge Maury of France.

The **1980** Olympics in Moscow, with the yachting events in **Tallinn**, Estonia suffered from the boycott initiated by the United States. A number of potential winners were excluded from the start. Some of those who came felt uncomfortable within the narrow limits of the strict organisation and performed poorly. The favourites – Jochen Schümann, Mark Neeleman, Lasse Hjortnäs, and Minski Fabris – failed to collect the medals. Gold and silver went to the rank outsiders Esko Rechardt and Wolfgang Mayrhofer in front of the only successful favourite, Andrei Balashov, who won bronze.

The Games suffered once again from a boycott at the **1984** Olympics in Los Angeles, this time initiated by the USSR. So in **Long Beach** the favourites from the DDR, Poland and the USSR were excluded. In the Finn class the actual Olympic sailing was preceded by an undignified controversy after the US trials. John Bertrand was declared the representative only 24 hours before the first start. In that race he had a collision with the later gold medal winner Russell Coutts from New Zealand and was disqualified. Disregarding the mental strain of the qualification battle and the disqualification in the first race, Bertrand was leading after the fifth and sixth race. In the last race however, he lost the gold to Coutts, and Terry Neilson from Canada won bronze.

The **1988** Olympic Regatta was held in the Bay of **Pusan** in South Korea. The final winner, José Luis Doreste, who had competed in both the 1976 and 1980 Olympics, was disqualified in race four for a collision.

Top right: Paul Elvstrøm won the third of his four gold medals in Melbourne in 1956 • Above: The fleet in 1988 • Left: Russell Coutts won gold in 1984 in Long Beach

Left top to bottom: José Maria van der Ploeg in 1996 in Savannah • Jonas Høgh-Christensen leads the pack in 2004 in Athens • Ben Ainslie leading the medal race in Qingdao in 2008 • Right top to bottom: Hank Lammens in 1992 in Barcelona • Start in 2008 • Iain Percy took the gold in 2000 in Sydney

The silver medalist Peter Holmberg scored PMS in race four and one of the favourites, Lasse Hjortnäs, broke his mast in race two after winning the first race. These events really opened up the racing. Eventually John Cutler won the last two races to take the bronze. Larry Lemieux gave up a good position in the fifth race to rescue two Singapore 470 sailors from the water after one had lost contact with his boat and was awarded Pierre de Coubertin Medal for Sportsmanship for this feat. Once again the sailors had to use boats that were provided by the organisers.

Barcelona, Spain, produced generally light to moderate conditions for the 1992 Olympics. The Finn fleet was the deepest ever and it was generally agreed that anyone in the first 15 could win the gold and any one of the first 22 could win a race. The final winner, José Maria van der Ploeg, never scored worse than sixth and didn't have to sail the final race. The two favourites, Eric Mergenthaler and Glenn Bourke, performed poorly and finished 18th and 20th. Brian Ledbetter was one of the few consistent sailors and won the silver medal, while Craig Monk, from New Zealand, won the last race to snatch the bronze away from Stuart Childerley. Prior to the regatta, the IFA conducted a two-week training clinic for those countries desiring assistance.

When the numerically stronger Laser was bidding for Olympic status, many thought it would replace the Finn as the Olympic singlehander for men. This was not to be, and in 1996 in Savannah there were two singlehanded dinghies for men. This worked well, as it meant there were two classes for two different weight categories. The advance weather reports suggested a light wind regatta. In fact, thunderstorm activity resulted in some spectacular weather and strong winds. Poland's first-ever sailing medal was won by Mateusz Kusznierewicz with a race to spare, and this in spite of losing his watch early on in the series and using the clock on the starting boat instead. Sebastien Godefroid from Belgium took the silver while relative Olympic veteran Roy Heiner took the bronze on the last race.

GREAT BRITAIN

In Sydney, Australia, in 2000 Iain Percy won the first medal for Great Britain in the class since Charles Currey's silver in 1952. Sailing a very consistent series, he had it all wrapped up before the final race. Luca Devoti's silver was one of the most unexpected medals of the Games, while Fredrik Lööf's bronze had been a long time coming. For the first time ever the sailors had been allowed to bring their own hulls as well as rigs. Also of importance to the Finn sailors of the future, Ben Ainslie won his first Olympic gold medal in the Laser class. Two years later he announced his switch to the Finn, where he dominated for the next 10 years.

Ainslie started the 2004 Olympics in Athens with a high score and a disqualification after being protested for a port-starboard incident, but fought back with a string of top results to make a remarkable comeback. He led into the final race and stuck to silver medalist Rafael

Trujillo to assure his second gold medal. Mateusz Kusznierewicz picked up his second Finn medal after winning the final race and taking bronze.

In 2008 in Qingdao, China, Ainslie took his third Olympic gold after winning three races in generally very light winds and very strong tides. He also won the medal race in very strong winds, the first time that format had been used at the Olympics. Zach Railey was the surprise silver medal winner but didn't win a single race and neither did Guillaume Florent, who took the bronze away from Daniel Birgmark on the medal race result, both sailors ending up with the same points.

MONOTYPE

Up to 1948 the type of boat used as the Monotype or singlehander was changed for each Olympic Games. With the introduction of the Finn in 1952 this problem was solved. The Finn was designed as an Olympic singlehander that could be sailed worldwide and aspiring Olympic sailors could practise and develop the required skills prior to the Games. It has established strict class rules and regulations and because of this has proven to be a true Olympic class reflecting the Olympic spirit.

The class inspires intense devotion from sailors and fans across the world. The Finn is a modern racing machine, a highly evolved piece of kit with an outstanding tradition and an amazing culture. It has become a supreme ambassador for all that is great about Olympic sailing and has evolved into a modern classic that has produced some of the world's best sailors.

* This text has been edited, abridged and amended from an article by David Leach, Richard Creagh-Osborne, Georg Siebeck and Robert Deaves and originally published in FINNLOG and FINNatics by the International Finn Association.

TWO

PREVIEW OF THE FINN CLASS AT LONDON 2012 OLYMPIC GAMES

The road to Weymouth was paved with drama and great battles on the water. Top: Close racing in Perth • Above: Rafael Trujillo chases Jonas Høgh-Christensen in Perth • Left: Ben Ainslie and Pieter-Jan Postma at the 2011 Finn Gold Cup in Perth

THE FIRST RACE OF THE London 2012 Olympic Sailing Competition for the Finn Class was on Sunday 29 July. The Finn fleet consisted of 24 sailors from five continents and was one of the most competitive fleets ever mustered for an Olympic regatta. The Finns were the first class to race and would finish on the first medal race day on Sunday 5 August. But before then there was a lot of sailing to be done...

It was a deep field of talent. The fleet included four Olympic medalists, six former World or European champions and another seven championship medalists. Any of 14 sailors could arguably win a medal. There was also a healthy mix of youth and experience in the fleet with ages ranging from 19 to 48, while the average was 30.

Apart from GBR as host nation, the first 18 nations qualified for a place in Weymouth at the Perth 2011 ISAF Sailing World Championships. These were AUS, BRA, CAN, CRO, DEN, ESP, EST, FIN, FRA, GRE, ITA, NED, NZL, RUS, SLO, SWE, UKR and USA.

Six more places were up for grabs at the J.P. Morgan Asset Management Finn Gold Cup in Falmouth in May 2012 and five of these places finally went to AUT, CHN, CZE, POL and TUR. Although Germany qualified, the German Federation decided not to make an entry into the Finn class and the place was lost to the class.

Ten sailors were sailing their first Olympics, seven were sailing their second, three were sailing their third and two were sailing their fourth and fifth Olympics. The only one sailing his fifth in the Finn was the reigning Masters World Champion, Michael Maier, who has probably sailed more miles in a Finn than anyone else in history.

EXPERIENCE

While Maier was the oldest by nine years, the youngest was 19-year-old Jorge Zarif. In 2009 on Lake Balaton he won the Junior World Championship – the Jorg Bruder Silver Cup – and hoped that the Weymouth experience in 2012 would stand him in good stead for the 2016 Olympics on home waters.

Without doubt the favourite was always going to be Ben Ainslie. Though he had shown everyone the occasional chink in his armour over the previous year, he was still the man everyone needed to beat, and beating him was never going to be easy. Everyone knew that if he won in Weymouth he would go down in history as the most successful Olympic sailor ever, taking that accolade from another Finn great, Paul Elvstrøm.

Whatever else happened, Ainslie was gong to be the story of the week. He had previously stated that anything else but gold would be a disaster, so he was bound to make the headlines, winning or not. He reflected, *"...a home Olympics makes it very special. I was in Trafalgar*

Square when they announced that London had won the bid for 2012. The atmosphere was electric and that's when I decided I wanted to continue my Olympic career and be a part of it. It is the most important regatta in my life right now, but they were all important to get to this point. I guess I have had more time to prepare for it, and I have had to, as the home competition has been tougher and the venue is also tough strategically."

But with such a talented pool of sailors, victory was not a given and he would have to work incredibly hard for it. More than half the fleet were quite capable of denying Ainslie a dream result and they wanted to be there just as much as he did. One man who knew that only too well was the 2008 silver medalist Zach Railey. In 2008 he was the only man who could beat Ainslie going into the medal race, but had the door firmly shut in his face by the determined Brit. Ever the optimist, Railey summed up the competition in 2012, *"These are the best Finn sailors in the world going head to head at their best and that is the exact situation I want to put myself into and see where I come out in the end. It is the ultimate test and I can't wait for it to begin."*

"I race every race from a clean slate. I do not worry about the end result until the regatta takes me there. If I am beaten by someone because they were better than I was I can accept that, but I cannot accept beating myself. The athletes always get better and better and smarter and smarter. It is amazing the progress you see over just a four-year period. You have to constantly keep making improvements or you get left behind."

CHALLENGES

The other main challenges were expected to come from Pieter-Jan Postma, who took bronze in the test event and silver at the 2011 world championship; Jonathan Lobert, who took silver at the test event; Ivan Kljakovic Gaspic, double European Champion and always hovering around the top of the fleet; and Rafael Trujillo, the silver medalist from the 2004 Olympics and the 2007 World Champion, though he'd had an inconsistent 2012 season in the lead-up to the Games.

Double World Champion Jonas Høgh-Christensen considered himself something of a dark horse, though he was anything but that. Although he hadn't won anything since returning to the class in 2011, he was clearly on the pace and gunning for a third chance at a medal. He described the challenge. *"I think the whole fleet is fitter, stronger and have improved their technique a lot. I don't have a lot of pressure as I am not one of the favourites to take a medal. Probably more a dark horse, but I think this could end up playing in my favour. I am fresh and really pushing hard all the way. But seeing the last 10 months' hard work come together with me performing my personal best, that will be the biggest satisfaction. I am truly blessed to have gotten another chance to do well at the Olympics and I will do my best to make the most of it."*

Another strong challenger was the double Laser medalist Vasilij Zbogar. Having moved into the class in 2010 he made an immediate impact, culminating in a silver medal at the 2012 Europeans in Scarlino. Between then and the Games he focused on training rather than regattas, so remained a bit of an unknown quantity.

Other potential race winners included Hyeres winner Brendan Casey, Kiel Week winner Deniss Karpak, Tapio Nirkko, Dan Slater and Daniel Birgmark, while some of the youngsters such as Greg Douglas, Ioannis Mitakis, Piotr Kula and Alican Kaynar had all made their mark in one way or another and could upset the apple cart if things went their way.

DEMANDING

Mitakis was the current European Champion, but was realistic about his chances. He said, *"I only started sailing the Finn in 2009 after realising that I had become too big for the Laser, so it was really demanding to qualify both my country and myself in only two years. I would be quite satisfied with a place in the top 10."*

One of the youngest was 22-year-old Greg Douglas, though he was sailing his second Olympics; the first was in a Laser for Barbados in 2008. *"It means so much to me to be sailing at the Olympics this year. I have been working very hard for this over the last three years. My goal is just to sail my best and show these guys what I can do. I am very excited for the event because anything can happen and it will be a great all-round test of sailing."*

At 34, Florian Raudaschl was finally sailing his first Olympics, following in his father's footsteps. Hubert Raudaschl won silver in the Finn in 1968. *"I tried it before [in 2004 and 2008] and was not sent because of our tough national criteria. I am very proud of my father, especially when I hear the different stories of him from other sailors. But to be honest, when you sail yourself and try to do a good regatta you do not think of this at all."*

"My goal is basically trying to do my best at the Olympic regatta. For the first time I have spent nearly as much time training as the other sailors do. That feels very good and even when the weather and wind situation in Weymouth are not my favourite ones, I really start liking the place. The whole Olympic atmosphere seems to come closer and closer and I try to enjoy this great time."

The Finn programme would begin on Sunday 29 July and would end with the medal race on Sunday 5 August. Reserve days were scheduled for Wednesday 1, Saturday 4 and Monday 6 August.

THREE
PORTRAIT OF THE LONDON 2012 FINN FLEET: 24 SAILORS, ONE GOAL

THE 24-STRONG FLEET THAT TOOK PART IN THE LONDON 2012 OLYMPIC SAILING COMPETITION WAS FULL OF TALENTED SAILORS WITH A WIDE RANGE OF AGES AND EXPERIENCE. SOME WERE SAILING THEIR FIFTH OLYMPICS, WHILE FOR OTHERS IT WAS THEIR FIRST FORAY ON THE OLYMPIC STAGE. BUT ALL WERE DETERMINED, FOCUSED AND SINGLE-MINDED. IT WOULD BE THE CULMINATION OF FOUR YEARS' HARD WORK, BUT ONLY THREE WOULD TAKE HOME THE MEDALS. HERE WE TAKE AN IN-DEPTH LOOK AT ALL OF THEM, THEIR HISTORY, THEIR POTENTIAL, THEIR STRONG POINTS AND THE LIKELY MEDAL PROSPECTS.

Left: Ivan Kljakovic Gaspic finished as runner-up at the 2012 Europeans in Scarlino and fourth at the 2012 Finn Gold Cup in Falmouth in the run-up to London 2012 • Above: Greg Douglas at the 2010 Finn Gold Cup in San Francisco

1. BRENDAN CASEY (AUS)
Age: 35 • World Ranking (highest): 7 (7)
Previous Olympics: None
Best Results: 2010 Finn Gold Cup (10)
2012 Results: Europeans (34), Finn Gold Cup (13), Palma (19), Hyeres (1), Weymouth (14), Kiel (2)

Brendan Casey is a very experienced sailor who had tried and failed several times to qualify for the Olympics and had now finally made it. He had won the Laser Radial World Championships in 1995 and 1996 before switching to the Laser. After failing to qualify in 2000 and 2004 he switched to the Finn in 2006 and won the Australian Championship, but again missed out on a spot in the 2008 Olympic team. He took a few years out and returned in 2010 to place 10th at the Finn Gold Cup in San Francisco. Results came, but he still had to prove himself to the selectors. His chance came in Hyeres in 2012, winning the last two races, including the very windy medal race, to win the regatta and his place in London. He just couldn't believe he had finally done it, 17 years after that first title.

2. FLORIAN RAUDASCHL (AUT)
Age: 34 • World Ranking (highest): 25 (19)
Previous Olympics: None
Best Results: 2006 Finn Gold Cup (16), 2009 Finn Gold Cup (18)
2012 Results: Europeans (14), Finn Gold Cup (23), Palma (32), Hyeres (17), Weymouth (25)

After trying for many years, Raudaschl finally made it to the Olympics to follow in the footsteps of his father's illustrious career. (Hubert Raudaschl had competed in more Olympics than any other athlete so far.) Working in the family sailmaking business, he had probably spent less time in the boat than most of his competitors in recent years, but during 2012 had put in some hard work in early in the year and the results started coming. Raudaschl has been campaigning a Finn since 1999 and while he performed well in the minor regattas, his two 10th places at Kiel Week in 2011 and 2010 were his only top 10 at Grade 1 regattas since 2008.

3. JORGE ZARIF (BRA)
Age: 19 • World Ranking (highest): 39 (35)
Previous Olympics: None
Best Results: 2009 Junior World Champion
2012 Results: Finn Gold Cup (34), Hyeres (19), Weymouth (20)

The youngest sailor in the Finn fleet at just 19, Zarif is the son of the late Jorge Zarif Zeto, who competed in the Finn in both the 1984 and 1988 Olympics, where he finished eighth and 19th. Sure to be a contender in his home Olympics in 2016, he was looking to gain experience and insight into the Olympics in 2012. However, he is a clever and hungry young sailor who had put in a few good results and set his goal for 2012 as getting into the medal race, with the podium in his sights for 2016 in Rio. Zarif has been competing in the Finn internationally since 2009 and in Brazil since 2008 when he was just 15 years old.

4. GREG DOUGLAS (CAN)

Age: 22 • World Ranking (highest): 27 (27)
Previous Olympics: 2008 Laser (43)
Best Results: 2012 Miami (3), 2011 Medemblik (8)
2012 Results: Finn Gold Cup (14), Palma (18), Weymouth (11)

Sailed the 2008 Olympics in the Laser for Barbados and finished last. Then switched allegiance to Canada, where he was trained by 2008 Olympian Chris Cook and started to bring in some encouraging results. Cook, who placed fifth in China, then returned to the Finn in 2011 and went up against his trainee in the Canadian Olympic trials. Douglas thought he had lost the trials in Falmouth after Cook surged ahead; but then, in a twist of fate, Cook got sick, retired from the regatta and Douglas got the 2012 ticket. Proved he can handle big conditions in Falmouth and improving all the time. Big, strong and very focused.

5. LEI GONG (CHN)

Age: 29 • World Ranking (highest): 59 (59)
Previous Olympics: None
Best Results: 2011 Gold Cup (35), Olympic Test Event (27), 2011 Medemblik (27)
2012 Results: Finn Gold Cup (30)

Sailed only a handful of regattas during this cycle after failing to qualify as China's representative in 2008. Finished one off the bottom at the 2011 Olympic Test Event, but clearly improved in the intervening months with a 30th at the 2012 Finn Gold Cup in Falmouth, where he qualified China for the Olympics. While China does have a core of Finn sailors, they rarely appear at international events. Gong is no exception having sailed only eight ranking events since 2004. He went into the Olympics as the lowest ranked sailor. His first international event was the Europeans in 2004 where he picked up the bronze medal in the Junior European championship behind Oleksiy Borysov from Ukraine and Tapio Nirkko from Finland, who both also competed at Weymouth.

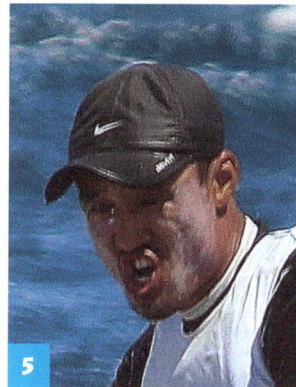

6. IVAN KLJAKOVIĆ GAŠPIĆ (CRO)

Age: 28 • World Ranking (highest): 3 (1)
Previous Olympics: 2008 (8)
Best Results: European Champion 2009, 2010; 2009 Finn Gold Cup (3)
2012 Results: Europeans (3), Finn Gold Cup (4), Weymouth (9)

A well rounded sailor with a good chance at a medal, Kljakovic Gaspic is one of the most consistent sailors on the circuit and is regularly at the front of international fleets. In China he finished in eighth place despite showing promise by nearly winning the 2007 test event. Since then he has matured as a sailor and put numerous regatta wins under his belt including the European Championship in 2009 and 2010. Over the year prior to the Games he had strengthened his armoury by improving his strong wind speed, as shown in his fourth place at the 2012 Finn Gold Cup in Falmouth. Earlier in the year he picked up the bronze at the light wind Europeans, though like most of the fleet he had done only a few regattas in what was a very busy early season.

Top to bottom: Jonathan Lobert at the Olympic Test Event in Weymouth in 2011 • Tapio Nirkko at the 2011 Finn Gold Cup in Perth • Jonas Høgh-Christensen on his way to fourth in Perth • Deniss Karpak ended up eighth in Perth

7. MICHAEL MAIER (CZE)

Age: 48 • World Ranking (highest): 19 (2)
Previous Olympics: 1996 (14), 2000 (19), 2004 (15), 2008 (25)
Best Results: 2000 Finn Gold Cup (5), 2009 Finn Gold Cup (15)
2012 Results: Finn Gold Cup (24), Hyeres (8), Weymouth (24)

The grand master of the Finn fleet, having just won his fourth Finn World Masters title, Maier was the oldest sailor in the Finn fleet at 48 and also the most experienced. This would be his fifth Olympics, all of them in the Finn. Maier has been campaigning Finns since the early 1980s and before many of the current fleet were even born. His debut event was the 1982 European Championship at the age of just 16. Thirty-two years later he is still going strong and just can't seem to let it go. He is still very competitive upwind but struggles downwind in the free pumping conditions.

8. JONAS HØGH-CHRISTENSEN (DEN)

Age: 31 • World Ranking (highest): 10 (1)
Previous Olympics: 2004 (9), 2008 (6)
Best Results: World Champion 2006, 2009
2012 Results: Finn Gold Cup (3), Palma (8), Weymouth (12)

After winning the 2006 Finn Gold Cup and picking up the bronze at the 2008 Finn Gold Cup, Høgh-Christensen went into the 2008 Olympics as one of the firm medal favourites. However things never really went his way. He did stage a late recovery to finish sixth, but that was a long way from where he wanted to be. He almost gave up, took a year off and came back, unprepared but fresh, to win the 2009 Finn Gold Cup on home waters. An on-off campaign ended in November 2011 when he started full-time again and the results gradually came. For 2012 he was right back at the top and would be a serious contender for a medal again. This was his third Olympics in the Finn.

9. RAFAEL TRUJILLO (ESP)

Age: 36 • World Ranking (highest): 1 (1)
Previous Olympics: 2000 Star (8), 2004 (2), 2008 (9)
Best Result: World Champion 2007
2012 Results: Europeans (10), Finn Gold Cup (18), Palma (21), Hyeres (2), Weymouth (10)

For Trujillo, one of the most experienced sailors in the fleet, London 2012 was his fourth Olympics and the third in the Finn. He picked up a silver medal in Athens in 2004 and then just made the medal race in China in 2008. He won the 2007 Finn Gold Cup after twice finishing second, losing the title on the final day, and claimed another runner-up place in 2010. Since then he has struggled with form, though he did finish fifth at the 2011 Finn Gold Cup. In 2012 he placed 10th at the Europeans and 18th at the Finn Gold Cup. Trujillo is a big, strong sailor who prefers breezy conditions and was certainly good enough to win another medal. He also went into the Olympics as the new world number one ranked sailor.

10. DENISS KARPAK (EST)

Age: 26 • World Ranking (highest): 2 (1)
Previous Olympics: 2008 Laser (24)
Best Results: 2011 Finn Gold Cup (8)
2012 Results: Finn Gold Cup (11), Europeans (6), Hyeres (4), Weymouth (15)

After sailing the 2008 Olympics in the Laser he moved straight into the Finn and has made steady progress ever since. He qualified for the 2012 Olympics after a great performance in Perth and won Kiel Week heading into the Games. A consistent year attending most of the major events also meant he briefly rose to the number one spot in the world rankings in June 2012. A tall, athletic figure, he had occasionally struggled in the really windy conditions, losing Hyeres in 2012 and finishing out of the medals after the medal race was sailed in 30 knots. Generally he has continually improved and was definitely top 10 material and a possible for a surprise medal. Karpak won the Sailor of the Year in Estonia from 2005-11 and the Best Young Athlete of the Year in Estonia in 2007.

11. TAPIO NIRKKO (FIN)

Age: 27 • World Ranking (highest): 17 (7)
Previous Olympics: 2008 (18)
Best Results: 2011 Finn Gold Cup (12), 2009 Europeans (2)
2012 Results: Finn Gold Cup (5), Palma (14), Weymouth (16)

For Nirkko, the only internationally competitive Finnish Finn sailor, this was his second Olympics after a disappointing regatta in China, where he placed 18th. Since then he has had a few moments of brilliance, picking up the silver medal at the 2009 Europeans and winning races here and there, generally in windy conditions. A tall and strong sailor, he has finally started to add some consistency and some promise to his regattas, something that has been lacking in recent years. He sailed his best Finn Gold Cup ever in May 2012 to place fifth, so if he maintained form he was expected to be well inside the top 10 come medal race day.

12. JONATHAN LOBERT (FRA)

Age: 27 • World Ranking (highest): 12 (6)
Previous Olympics: None
Best Results: Olympic Test Event (2), 2011 Finn Gold Cup (6)
2012 Results: Finn Gold Cup (15), Palma (23), Weymouth (7)

A silver medal at the Olympic Test Event in 2011 was the culmination of steady progress over the previous few years. Lobert won his selection for the Olympics after the 2011 Finn Gold Cup against training partner Thomas Le Breton. He has a very athletic style in the boat, especially downwind, and was expected to do well at the Olympics. He hadn't quite repeated his test event form since August 2011 but was always pushing the leaders. He first moved into the Finn in early 2007 after outgrowing the Laser. He was a certain favourite for a medal at the Olympics based on past performance, especially as he always seemed to produce his best in Weymouth.

Top to bottom: Pieter-Jan Postma at the 2011 Finn Gold Cup in Perth • Ben Ainslie leads away at the Olympic Test Event in Weymouth in 2011 • Ioannis Mitakis won the European Championship in Scarlino in 2012 • Filippo Baldassari at the 2012 Europeans

13. BEN AINSLIE (GBR)

Age: 35 • World Ranking (highest): 18 (1)
Previous Olympics: 2008 (1), 2004 (1), Laser: 2000 (1), 1996 (2)
Best Results: World Champion 2002-5, 2008, 2012
2012 Results: Finn Gold Cup (1), Palma (1), Weymouth (2)

After winning gold in 2008 there was much speculation whether Ainslie would return, but the demise of Team Origin made the decision easy and he returned to full-time Finn sailing in 2010. After being unbeaten since 2004, his greatest threat came from Giles Scott and in the UK trials the 2011 Skandia Sail for Gold was the decisive regatta for them both. Ainslie won and went on to dominate the Olympic Test Event to win selection. The controversial 2011 Finn Gold Cup was followed by a back operation, but he bounced back to dominate Palma and the 2012 Finn Gold Cup. Ainslie was going for a record fourth gold medal, which together with a silver from 1996, would make him the most successful Olympic sailor of all time. He was the absolute favourite to win gold.

14. IOANNIS MITAKIS (GRE)

Age: 23 • World Ranking (highest): 13 (11)
Previous Olympics: None
Best Results: 2011 Finn Gold Cup (20), 2010 Europeans (12)
2012 Results: Europeans (1), Athens (1), Weymouth (26)

Mitakis won the 2012 European Championship out of nowhere in very light and shifty winds. He first appeared in a Finn in 2009 and took the Junior European title in Bulgaria with ease. The following year he won it again in Croatia, this time also finishing 12th overall in the senior fleet. Then in 2010 he finished as runner-up in the Silver Cup in San Francisco. A clearly talented sailor, he was widely considered to be a serious challenger in 2016, but he didn't want to wait that long. One of the lightest sailors in the fleet, he often struggled when it was windy, but produced his best in lighter conditions. His biggest enemy was perhaps lack of regatta practice during 2012.

15. FILIPPO BALDASSARI (ITA)

Age: 24 • World Ranking (highest): 40 (27)
Previous Olympics: None
Best Results: 2011 Finn Gold Cup (24), 2011 Hyeres (10)
2012 Results: Europeans (4), Palma (13), Weymouth (21)

The first sailor to qualify for the Olympics, Baldassari won the Italian national trials in April 2011. He had made steady progress after securing his place and gradually moved up the rankings, including an impressive fourth overall at the light wind 2011 Europeans in Italy. He was also one of a few sailors who skipped the 2011 Finn Gold Cup to take a break from the hectic early season. His 10th place last year in Hyeres was Baldassari's only top 10 placing at a Sailing World Cup or Grade 1 event since he switched to the Finn from the Laser in 2009.

16. PIETER-JAN POSTMA (NED)

Age: 30 • World Ranking (highest): 4 (2)
Previous Olympics: 2008 (14)
Best Results: 2007 Finn Gold Cup (2), 2011 Finn Gold Cup (2)
2012 Results: Finn Gold Cup (9), Europeans (7), Palma (15), Medemblik (3),
Weymouth (3)

Postma picked up the silver medal at the Finn Gold Cup and the Pre-Olympics in 2007 and then had a disastrous Olympics in 2008, failing to even make the medal race. After a few years taking it easy and studying he is now right back in contention with a bronze at the 2011 Olympic Test Event and a silver at the 2011 Finn Gold Cup. He placed seventh at the Europeans after being one of the favourites; and the spectre of national qualification perhaps played its part in a scrappy 2012 Finn Gold Cup where he salvaged a ninth. However, he later pulled a third out of the bag at the 2012 Skandia Sail for Gold Regatta. As a fast and clever sailor he would be a clear medal contender at the Games.

17. DAN SLATER (NZL)

Age: 36 • World Ranking (highest): 15 (2)
Previous Olympics: 2000 49er (8), 2008 (12)
Best Results: Finn Gold Cup: 2008 (6), 2008 (2), 2009 (7)
2012 Results: Finn Gold Cup (16), Palma (5), Hyeres (5)

Third Olympics for Dan Slater after sailing a 49er in 2000 and finishing a very disappointing 12th in 2008 in the Finn, after having been runner-up in the 2008 Finn Gold Cup. Selected late by New Zealand Yachting, he was perhaps a bit short on training but his experience of the arena and the fleet easily gave him top 10 potential and he would be in with a shot at the medals. A very experienced sailor, he also campaigned the Laser for the 1996 and 2004 Olympics but failed to get selected. Finally switched to the Finn in 2005 and immediately made his mark with a silver medal at the 2005 European Championships. He had won several Grade 1 regattas in recent years and surely had the ability and potential to medal.

18. PIOTR KULA (POL)

Age: 25 • World Ranking (highest): 28 (13)
Previous Olympics: None
Best Results: 2011 Finn Gold Cup (23), 2011 Medemblik (7)
2012 Results: Gold Cup (6), Palma (11), Hyeres (12), Weymouth (17)

Won a very close Polish trials against the 2008 Olympian Rafal Szukiel and placed a very creditable sixth overall at the 2012 Finn Gold Cup, which clearly showed his talent. He struggled with a knee injury since late 2011, which kept him out of the 2011 Finn Gold Cup in Perth, but proved during 2012 he had the tenacity and the determination to race at the highest level. The Poles failed to qualify for the Olympics in Perth so it came down to Falmouth in addition to being their final selection trials. Kula was clearly on a mission all week and produced the best results of his career to date.

Top to bottom: Eduard Skornyakov at the 2011 Olympic Test Event in Weymouth • Zach Railey at the test event • Vasilij Zbogar at the 2011 Finn Gold Cup in Perth • Daniel Birgmark in big waves at the 2011 test event

19. EDUARD SKORNYAKOV (RUS)

Age: 31 • World Ranking (highest): 14 (7)
Previous Olympics: 2008 (17)
Best Results: 2010 Hyeres (10), 2011 Fin Gold Cup (33)
2012 Results: Finn Gold Cup (17), Europeans (11), Palma (22), Hyeres (6), Weymouth (27)

First appeared on the Finn scene in 2007 when he was the surprise winner of the European Championships on Lake Balaton in Hungary, in similar conditions to his home waters on the lakes in Moscow. Since then he never got close to repeating that performance but had started to make headway into the top of the fleet. After a brief spell in the Laser and the 49er he moved into the Finn in early 2007. His European title was only his third major regatta in the class. Since then he had made the top 10 only on a handful of occasions, but a sixth in Hyeres in 2012 proved that he was on the right track.

20. VASILIJ ŽBOGAR (SLO)

Age: 36 • World Ranking (highest): 13 (4)
Previous Olympics: Laser 2000 (19), 2004 (3), 2008 (2)
Best Results: 2011 Europeans (6), 2011 Finn Gold Cup (13)
2012 Results: Europeans (2), Palma (7), Hyeres (3)

Won a very aggressive trials again the 2004 and 2008 Olympian Gasper Vincec. Zbogar is a seasoned Olympian having competed in three Games in the Laser already and picked up a bronze and a silver in that class. He took the silver medal at the 2012 Europeans and then dominated the close of the Slovenian trials before taking some time out. Going into the Olympics he hadn't raced in a competitive regatta since Hyeres. After his first medal in 2004 he was declared Slovenian Sportsman of the Year. He switched to the Finn in 2010 and made steady progress. Capable of a top 10 result and perhaps fighting for a medal come the end of the event.

21. DANIEL BIRGMARK (SWE)

Age: 39 • World Ranking (highest): 9 (4)
Previous Olympics: 2004 (14), 2008 (4)
Best Results: 2011 Europeans (3), 2009 Finn Gold Cup (5)
2012 Results: Finn Gold Cup (12), Palma (6), Weymouth (8)

After missing out in the Laser class in 2004, Birgmark switched to the Finn, which was a much better fit for his size and weight, and immediately qualified for Athens. After a 14th in 2004, he lost the bronze medal at the Olympics in 2008 on the tie break after the medal race. His best result since 2008 was a bronze medal at the 2010 Europeans. Struggled for form in 2012, though he had a history of sailing well in medal races, and almost won the medal race at the 2012 Skandia Sail for Gold Regatta. A very consistent, steady and calm sailor who is always there or thereabouts. It was probably his last Olympics in the Finn, so he was very determined to make it count.

22. ALICAN KAYNAR (TUR)

Age: 23 • World Ranking (highest): 35 (35)
Previous Olympics: None
Best Results: 2011 Finn Gold Cup (52), 2011 Europeans (33)
2012 Results: Europeans (12), Gold Cup (29), Hyeres (21), Weymouth (28)

Sailed the 2009 Europeans and then switched full-time to the Finn in 2010 after many years in the Laser. Won the Turkish trials after the 2012 Finn Gold Cup in Falmouth after sailing well to beat the long-time Finn sailor Akif Muslubus. Kaynar had shown steady improvement since 2010 but had yet to break through very often. One highlight was the 2012 European Championship in Scarlino, Italy, where he won a race and finished 12th overall. Still relatively small compared with the rest of the fleet but clearly quick in light winds.

23. OLEKSIY BORYSOV (UKR)

Age: 29 • World Ranking (highest): 24 (15)
Previous Olympics: None
Best Results: 2011 Finn Gold Cup (22) 2011 Europeans (20)
2012 Results: Finn Gold Cup (21), Palma (24), Hyeres (16), Weymouth (34)

Having missed out on qualifying for the 2008 Olympics by just one place, this time around Borysov qualified at the first attempt in Perth to secure his place in Weymouth. Has been sailing the Finn internationally since 2004 and has won only one major ranking event, the 2011 Sail Melbourne, in that time. He also placed second in Kiel Week in 2010. One of only two dinghy sailors representing Ukraine in Weymouth (the other is in the Laser), Borysov unfortunately was forced to miss the 2011 Skandia Sail for Gold and the 2011 Olympic Test Event owing to lack of financial support.

24. ZACH RAILEY (USA)

Age: 28 • World Ranking (highest): 8 (1)
Previous Olympics: 2008 (2)
Best Results: 2009 Finn Gold Cup (2), 2011 Finn Gold Cup (9)
2012 Results: Finn Gold Cup (10), Miami (1), Palma (2), Weymouth (4)

Against all expectations Railey won the silver medal in China and had been trying to live up to his billing ever since. The closest he got was a silver at the 2009 Finn Gold Cup, losing the title on the medal race. He had picked up various medals at several Sailing World Cup events and posted a solid fourth place at the 2012 Skandia Sail for Gold Regatta. Though not the biggest sailor in the fleet in the past he produced some of his best results at windy regattas, as well as at light wind venues such as Qingdao. A very thoughtful, analytical sailor, he had it well within his ability to pick up another medal in Weymouth.

FOUR

ZACH RAILEY INTERVIEW
'LIVING THE DREAM'

Top and left: Zach Railey at the 2011 Finn Gold Cup in Perth where he placed ninth • Above: At the 2010 Finn Gold Cup in San Francisco where he finished fourth

GOING INTO THE 2008 OLYMPICS Zach Railey was a relative unknown. He was one of the newest sailors in the class and was not really expected to win a medal. However, his consistency in the early days left him leading the regatta and he was suddenly the centre of attention. As the event closed out he held his cool despite being match raced out of the first attempt to get the medal race away by the eventual gold medalist Ben Ainslie. Zach eventually took silver a day later when it was re-sailed in strong winds and big seas. It was a day that changed his life and the realisation of an ambition that started when he was 12.

Four years later he was the US Team Captain and a role model for a generation of young sailors. He started sailing at age eight, following a suggestion from his family dentist to try summer sailing classes. Sailing Optimists until he was almost 13, he switched to the Radial and then the Laser, but outgrew each boat in turn. Then Chris Cook from Canada asked Zach to sail with him one day in a Finn and he has been hooked ever since.

NEW APPROACH

Last time around, the US Olympic trials was a single winner-takes-all regatta. Like many elements of the new US approach to Olympic sailing, the trials system was radically changed; this time several major regattas were used as indicators.

Railey said, *"I like the new format as it measures you against the international competition you will race against at the Olympics. It also allows you to continue on the Olympic circuit without having to come home and concentrate on a trials event in the middle of the season. Overall, I think this was a huge success and I think it should be the way forward for our qualifications for 2016 and beyond. There may have to be some different regattas used next time but the general idea is a huge success."*

While winning the silver in China was a massive achievement by any standards, bettering that colour in Weymouth was an even bigger challenge, yet Zach was never negative about his chances and always focused on what he was able to control.

"It is a big ask to qualify for the Olympics let alone then medal or win. This is hard and you are competing against the best in the world. That

being said, I am confident in my abilities and confident in the training and planning that has gone into the last four years. These are the best Finn sailors in the world going head to head at their best and that is the exact situation I want to put myself into and see where I come out in the end. It is the ultimate test and I can't wait for it to begin."

"I race every race from a clean slate. I do not worry about the end result until the regatta takes me there. My job is to go out and post the best results that I can in each race and see how the regatta unfolds. Every event is different and there is no way to predict what will happen, so I worry about me and let the results speak for themselves. If I am beaten by someone because they were better than I was, I can accept that, but I cannot accept beating myself."

PROGRESS

"The athletes always get better and better and smarter and smarter. It is amazing the progress you see over just a four-year period. You have to constantly keep making improvements or you get left behind. I think physically this four years has made a huge difference as I am now almost 40 pounds heavier than when I was in China. That has taken a lot of work and I am very proud of getting my body ready for the conditions in Weymouth.

"I also think the addition of the free pumping rule to 10 knots has made the boat much more physically gruelling and has really pushed the class forward in terms of a true athletic test."

Since 2008 Zach had matured as a Finn sailor and had achieved a reasonable level of success on the circuit. A year after the Olympic medal he took another silver, this time at the Finn Gold Cup in Copenhagen, and very nearly won the world title.

In subsequent years he picked up several medals including a silver at Hyeres in 2011 and a silver at Palma in 2012. He also took gold, albeit in a smaller fleet at Miami in 2012. Top 10 places at four world championships is evidence enough that he was a force to be reckoned with, as well as a record that not many other Finn sailors in Weymouth could match.

CHALLENGE

"I like to challenge myself. For me that means sailing against the best and trying to beat the best. For sailing, that means the Olympics, Volvo Ocean Race or the America's Cup. I fell in love with the Olympics in 1996 when Atlanta hosted the Olympic Games. I was 12 years old and remember watching Michael Johnson win the 200 metres on TV and thought one day I could be there. I'm living the dream right now."

"You have to be very dedicated to do an Olympic campaign, so dedicated that most people see it as being selfish. I don't think of myself as selfish but as a person who has a dream and knows that there are people out there who will help me achieve my dream. I know that I have given up so much to get to this point, but I am perfectly content with the decision to do so because I am doing exactly what I have always wanted to do with my life."

"I know that most people will not understand why you would sacrifice so much, but I have a great support system and they sometimes don't understand it themselves, but they will always stand by me no matter what sacrifices have to be made. One of my favourite quotes is: 'Talent is common. Disciplined talent is rare' I believe that I am a very disciplined person."

What about the sacrifices? "My personal life has taken the biggest toll. I have an amazing family who are incredibly supportive of what I do, and also what my sister Paige does, and we have both made it to the Olympics in 2012 because of our family support system. The number of relationships lost over the years because of being gone, doing so much training and travelling, are too many to count; but I would change nothing, it's all worth it, and those who have been there for the long haul are truly special to me."

Did winning an Olympic medal in 2008 change his life? "It certainly brought a lot more attention to me after 2008. That took some time for me to adjust to afterwards. I think the greatest thing about it was the opportunities I was given to achieve some non-sailing goals like the OliviaLives Charity (OliviaLives.com) which is a huge accomplishment for Paige, myself, our entire family and all of the supporters who help make it a success. "

"Also, becoming a role model for younger sailors to show them that they can do exactly what I have done. Expectations, of course, have gone up and you accept that as part of the territory."

SILVER

In 2008 Zach was famously sailed out of the first attempt at the medal race in very light winds by a ruthless Ben Ainslie. They were both way behind the fleet when it was finally abandoned. When it was resailed a day later in strong winds, it was easier for Zach to sail his own race and secure the silver. What did he learn from that? "I think the biggest lesson from the experience is always to be prepared for any situation."

Getting the gear right is a crucial part of winning in the Finn as the rig can be tailored around particular body weights and sailing styles. "This is an area where I really learned a lot over the past four years. With my big weight change and the difference in my strength and techniques we changed my gear; but they are small changes like having a little bit stiffer mast in some areas. It is nothing that the other competitors have not done themselves."

"Most of it had to do with my weight gain and getting the correct bend in the mast to support the weight and strength I had added and then matching the sail to that mast. My gear in 2008 was for when I weighed 185 pounds and was for a light air venue. Now I am much larger and Weymouth is a very different venue so we needed to add some more strength to my equipment and power in the rig."

FREE PUMPING

Since 2008 the class had also introduced free pumping on offwind legs in winds over 10 knots and this had changed the game somewhat, favouring the tall, athletic sailors. Had there been a change in rig design or sail shape brought on by the free pumping rule? "I don't think there has been a change because of the pumping rule with equipment, but physically it's been a huge development of maintaining power while increasing your cardiovascular capacity. It's very hard to maintain both correctly and we have worked hard to get where I am at today."

At a venue like Weymouth, with many different conditions, how do you select the right gear? "Great question and I wish I knew 100 per cent the answer. I think you need to develop your gear for what conditions are most likely to be present but not totally specialise them in case there are a few days that are different. So you go with an all around set-up. Weymouth could be anything – we have seen it all there – but compared to China in 2008 it is a much windier and colder venue."

SUPERSTITIONS

Does he have any rituals or superstitions when racing? "I do have a few that mostly go back a long way. I always wear a University of Miami hat; I listen to the same song before going on the water, which no one knows, not even my family; and lastly I will not shave during a regatta except for the night before the medal race. So I guess I am superstitious – but they are fun."

What's planned after the Olympics? "I am really interested in the Volvo Ocean Race and want to do some more offshore sailing after the Olympics. Of course, the America's Cup has always been a dream and we will see if an opportunity presents itself there in the future."

"My big three in sailing have always been the Olympics, Volvo Ocean Race and the America's Cup. After 2012 we will see which one of those three I put my efforts toward but for now it's all about the Olympics."

And Finn sailing? "I love the Finn and I will always have one for sure and compete at events. As for doing another campaign in the Finn…"

When asked to pick three favourites for a medal? "This one is hard. I really think that there are about 10 guys who can make it happen and

be on the podium. To narrow it down to three is what the Olympics will tell us. Ask me again on 6 August."

And finally, what was he looking forward to the most as the Games approached? "Walking into the Opening Ceremony with my sister Paige. We have been dreaming of that moment since we were little kids. It's going to be a very special moment for both of us."

NOTE: These six interviews were all carried out in the final few weeks before the Games commenced and were released in the order they are shown on these pages. They provide a unique insight into the thought processes of these athletes as they prepared for the biggest regatta of their lives.

FIVE
JONATHAN LOBERT INTERVIEW
'GREAT EXPECTATIONS'

JONATHAN LOBERT WENT INTO THE London 2012 Olympic Sailing Competition with the expectations of a nation on his broad shoulders. After the 2008 Finn Class bronze medal was won by fellow French sailor Guillaume Florent, more French success was expected in 2012, with Jonathan's performance in recent years suggesting that another Finn medal was a distinct possibility.

In 2008 Florent beat Jonathan in the French trials before going on to win the bronze at the Olympics in China. At the time Jonathan was a relative newcomer to the Finn fleet, having moved into the class in 2007 after outgrowing the Laser. But he made steady progress and then in 2010 was suddenly the centre of attention as he led the fleet for much of that year's Skandia Sail for Gold Regatta - the event that saw the return of Ben Ainslie to the Finn fleet. Jonathan eventually ended up second to Giles Scott.

He lost his way a bit at the 2010 Finn Gold Cup in San Francisco, finishing 13th, some way behind his main competition for the Olympic berth, Thomas Le Breton, who placed fifth. At the end of the year, he won the 2010 Perth International Regatta; and then the following year Jonathan picked up the silver medal at the 2011 Olympic Test Event in Weymouth, a big step towards his eventual selection. A sixth place at the 2011 Finn Gold Cup in Perth sealed it for Jonathan and soon afterwards he was announced as the French choice for Weymouth.

RECORD

France does not have a great record in the Finn Class at the Olympics. Aside from Florent's bronze, France's only other medal was from Serge Maury, who struck gold in 1972 when the sailing events were in Kiel. So with Jonathan medaling in two of the four major events in Weymouth in the run-up to the Games, it is fair to say that he was expected to perform well. He had also usually saved his best for Weymouth.

Always very polite and modest, Jonathan put his success down to a team effort. "*I am very lucky because until the end of the preparation for the Games I had Thomas sailing with me and always pushing hard. My coach François [Le Castrec] is always helping me to stay on the track we have chosen together. Also with Tapio [Nirkko], Daniel [Birgmark] and Jokke [Wilenius] we have a great training group. I think all these people are very important to succeed.*"

"*I try to see this as a great chance to be a part of the Olympics and I would like to have no regrets about my sailing at the end of the*

Above: Jonathan Lobert on his way to the silver medal at the 2011 Olympic Test Event • Left: At the 2011 Finn Gold Cup in Perth

regatta. I will try my best as always. As it's my first Games, I am looking forward to feeling the atmosphere of this unique event."

PHYSIQUE

Jonathan's physique is ideally suited to the Finn. In a 2011 interview he said, *"I am very attracted by the Finn because I think the boat looks great; and this bunch of tall and strong guys is very friendly. I love the downwind with the free pumping. It is so exciting surfing the waves standing up in the boat and feeling this heavy boat becoming lighter and lighter as the speed increases. You need to be strong and you need to have a very good cardio, but for me the key is to feel the boat sliding on the water."*

"We can pump from 10 knots of wind, but when it's around 10 knots you need to have a perfect move to increase your speed. I think it's really good for the class because the sailing technique is improving all the time. And when people are watching the Finn they say, 'that's real sport!"

Attendance at many regattas was fairly low before the Games. He explained, *"I think it's always like this before the Games. Some guys are still in selections. The Falmouth Finn Festival was just after Hyeres, while the Europeans was on the other side of Europe to where we were training in Cadiz. I just try to be in good form when I go to the regattas to do my best."*

CAMPAIGN

What was the hardest part about the campaign this time around? *"The hardest part of the campaign has been the last six months since when I was selected. It took me a bit of time to get used to it."*

What makes the Olympics so special for him? *"In dinghy sailing it's the greatest regatta you can compete in. It's only every four years and when you are successful you are part of the history of your sport. But you need to be dedicated to it, you need to really enjoy what you are doing and you need to be a little bit crazy. But it's no sacrifice to me, because I love what I do."*

For many sailors, the final choice of gear can be a stressful time as well as a critical decision. For Jonathan this is far from the case. *"For me it's easy because I almost always use the same gear everywhere. I try to adapt myself and not the gear."*

"I will be using a Hit mast and a Wilke mast. I will use both but I have a better feeling with my Hit and I have the Wilke just in case. For my sails I will use a WB, of course. I love those sails and they are very well made. They are very fast in some conditions and I had good results in Weymouth with it."

"I haven't changed much over the past four years. I just fixed my Hit mast many times because it had a few cracks from the sails we were working with Jokke, Tapio and Daniel to improve in the strong wind and I think we did it pretty well."

How did he plan the lead up to the Games? *"Before it starts I just chill and try to be as bored as possible to be really happy to jump in my boat for the Games."*

"What is great about sailing is that you never know what could happen. It's also the only sport where a beginner can sometimes beat an Olympic champion in one race. This is why I think it's really open. The fleet is tight and a lot of guys can win."

After the Olympics? *"I think I will keep on sailing Finn but I would like to join a team in the America's Cup or in big boat sailing to learn to a different way of racing."*

"I would like to see faster races in the Olympics. I like the medal race format and I like the way they are sailing the 49er. This could be great for the Finns, something like we did in Perth close to the shore. A bit like what is happening in the Cup."

FAVOURITES

Jonathan was one of the few sailors interviewed who would be drawn on his medal favourites (apart from himself), *"Ben Ainslie, Pieter-Jan Postma and Jonas Høgh-Christensen."*

To end with another quote from the 2011 interview, Jonathan had said, *"The most important thing I learned in the Finn Class is that it is possible to sail like gentlemen – enemies on the water, but very good friends on the shore."*

There would be 24 enemies sailing Finns in Weymouth Bay, but more than a few friends on shore once the racing was over, whether or not a medal had been won.

SIX
IVAN KLJAKOVIC GASPIC
INTERVIEW
'ENJOYING EVERY MOMENT'

Top and middle: Ivan Kljakovic Gaspic struggled in the strong winds at the 2011 Finn Gold Cup in Perth to place 10th • Left: However he managed to finish fifth at the 2011 Olympic Test Event despite mainly strong winds

AFTER FINISHING EIGHTH AT THE 2008 Olympics, Ivan Kljakovic Gaspic did some serious winning. Over the next four years he won two European titles, four ISAF Sailing World Cup events and countless races at these and other regattas. He briefly rose to No.1 in the world rankings and went into the Olympics as the world No.3. He became one of the best Finn sailors in the world and a favourite to medal at every regatta he enters.

Ivan, better known as Bambi, first emerged in the Finn in 2005. He took the Junior World title the same year and gradually climbed to the top of the international fleet. Since then he has been a regular medal winner, but surprisingly has only ever medalled once at the Finn Gold Cup. He took the bronze in Vallensbaek, Denmark in 2009.

OPPOSITION

The main reason he cites for this was the number of big breeze venues, as he has generally been sailing at a lower-than-average weight. In spite of this he still made the Finn Gold Cup medal race in 2010 and 2011, though he was never really in the race for the title. Perhaps more importantly in terms of the Olympics, he won the Skandia Sail for Gold Regatta in 2010 against some serious opposition.

Going into 2012, he worked on his strong wind speed, resulting in a fourth place at the Finn Gold Cup in Falmouth, UK, after a very windy week. Ivan said he felt as complete a sailor as he had ever been.

Although awed by the prospect of sailing in Weymouth, he tried to keep a cool head and focus on the job in hand. *"It is for sure the biggest regatta of my life and it is hard to be cool with it. Anyway, I think it will be a great event and I will enjoy sailing this one like the best ever. This time around the major difference for me is that it has been much easier. I am older and more experienced and better prepared. I have had great training and my equipment is really good. And in terms of others, let's see what happens on the racing days."*

TRAINING

Like many competitors heading to the Olympics, he struggled to get to grips with the Weymouth conditions, despite winning there in 2010. He said this was perhaps one of the reasons that sailors have favoured training there rather than doing regattas. *"We all see Weymouth as a pretty special venue, so we are trying to sail there as much as possible.*

But my preparations are already done, so now I will just relax and wait for the gun."

He claimed not to have done much in the way of gear development, sticking to the gear he knew best. *"I just use ordinary kit and use it as best as I can. I think too drastic equipment changes can give you a headache. I had some softer masts, but now found a stiffer one to suit me better, especially in the stronger breeze."* As a result, he keeps his gear selection relatively simple. *"North Sails and Wilke masts because I like the feeling when I am using them."* However, he says that money has been the hardest part about the campaign this time around.

He also thinks the advent of free pumping at 10 knots has had an effect on the rig design. *"A bit stiffer mast gives you better power. So, yes, there was a bit of focus on that."*

FUTURE

What of the future? *"For sure sailing the Finn is a great game for me but I will take short break after August. I'd like to do some big boats in the future and then come back into the Finn for Rio."*

"I would like to see sailing becoming a more popular sport and bring it closer to the public. I think we need to make it more interesting, lively and faster. Perhaps a more risky game."

COMPETING

Kljakovic Gaspic says that for him, competing at the Olympics is all about the honour. However, there is a downside. *"I gave up all my free time and I have to be away from my family for long periods of time."* But he also thinks that determination and motivation are the principal qualities of being an successful Olympic campaigner.

His favourites for a medal included Vasilij Zbogar, Jonas Høgh-Christensen and Ben Ainslie, but did he expect Ainslie to win the regatta again? *"He is great sailor, but let's see results on the last day... that is sport."*

Finally, some advice for racing at Weymouth? *"Keep it simple and sail fast and smart."* But above all he was looking forward to *"Enjoying every moment of being an Olympian".*

SEVEN
JONAS HØGH-CHRISTENSEN INTERVIEW
'THIRD TIME LUCKY?'

OF ALL THE FINN SAILORS who competed in the 2012 Olympics, Jonas Høgh-Christensen had one of the toughest returns to form after effectively stepping out of the class for three years following a disappointing 2008 Olympics. In China he was one of the hot favourites for a medal, but he had a poor start before recovering to finish sixth, although that was still a long way from where he wanted to be. Perhaps it was nerves, perhaps it was just bad luck.

So he took some time out, put his sailing career on hold and focused on another career, in the music business. He returned briefly for the 2009 Finn Gold Cup in Vallensbaek, Denmark, where he stunned the Finn world to win his second Finn world title. Over the next two years he sailed the odd regatta to keep his hand in, until in November 2011 he returned to the class full-time for a third crack at an Olympic medal. This was seen by many as his best chance yet. He was relaxed, confident and fast. But it had been a physically hard route back to the top.

DIMENSIONS

"It was very, very hard to come back after such a long break. Physically and mentally it was a test of dimensions. My body was so out of shape and getting back to the mental state you need to be in to compete at this level was hard, too. My first regatta back in the boat was Hyeres regatta in 2011 and I just wasn't there. I sat down with my coach and made a plan to get back and instantly knew that it would be a hard challenge."

"To make another campaign was not planned and not even really something I had rumbling in my head. I liked sailing at the top level but had decided to move on with my life. In 2010 I was approached by our federation, which needed somebody to get some results because of a bad Danish season. I said I needed to test myself to see if it was even a possibility as it was crucial that I had the will to push as hard as needed and that the passion was still there. I tested myself at the 2010 Worlds and with a 14th I thought I had both the opportunity to do well again and the will and passion to push hard."

As usual, fitness was the hardest part of the comeback. *"I was very out of shape and three years in the music business had left its mark. I was 112 kg and super-unfit. Getting back into shape has been hard especially because I have been battling injuries all along the process."* He also felt there had been a major step change in the fitness of the fleet. *"I think the whole fleet is fitter, stronger and have improved*

Top: Jonas Høgh-Christensen placed fourth at the 2011 Finn Gold Cup in Perth • Middle: He finished eighth at the 2011 Olympic Test Event • Left: The 2012 Finn Gold Cup in Falmouth when he finished third.

their technique a lot. But I don't have a lot of pressure as I am not one of the favourites to take a medal. Probably more a dark horse. I think this could end up playing in my favour. But I am fresh and am really pushing hard all the way. I see some sailors that have already burned out. I did the same in 2008 in many ways and have learned from that."

The gear had also moved on. "When I returned it was obvious that the Brits were several steps ahead of everybody on gear. In the first race back in the boat I saw Ben sail a medal race going 0.3 knots and three degrees higher than everybody else. It made no sense. So we have worked hard to catch up. I did a mast development programme with Concept masts and sails with North. I think we have done well, but in this aspect another six months would have done wonders. I think people were pretty surprised when I showed up with a 3DL sail at Sail for Gold."

FULL CIRCLE

"I think we have come full circle and will be using a mix of new and old gear. But we did push the bar and I can say we found some magic on the way. What it is will show at the Games."

Unfortunately, Jonas broke his mast soon after this interview, so for a while he was unsure what he would use at the Olympics. "I was training in 20-25 knots. I am not sure what happened, but when I got in I could see that my mast had cracked halfway around, 25 cm above the gooseneck. I liked that mast and had a good reason to believe that it gave me an edge. We are in the process of fixing it and getting a lot of help from Luca [Devoti]. So a big thanks to him. I have my 2001 Wilke mast as back-up. I have used this mast forever and it has always done well. I have won two Worlds and had some top four finishes with that mast, so it is not a bad mast." Luckily the new mast was fixed in time for the start of the regatta.

On his preparation he said, "Focus on fitness is key and regattas can disrupt a good fitness programme. To do well you need to be fresh and this season you could do regattas back-to-back. For me a focus on keeping fresh and work on the gear was more important than racing. If I couldn't get on the same page as Ben, I would be racing for secondary positions."

Looking back at the 2008 Olympics, Jonas was clearly unhappy with his performance, but in hindsight felt there were some positives. "I think it was a hard regatta and luck was not on my side. When I finally got back on form the wind died and we didn't race."

"Going into the event I felt really prepared, but I was also nervous as I was one of the favourites. Sometimes you just don't have a good week and that happened to me. Looking back there are a couple of things I would change, but the experience has been a gift for this Games. My preparation for 2012 has been much shorter, though not too different. Get the equipment right, be in shape, be sharp. Off you go and do your best."

To win a medal the top 10 would face the toughest challenge yet in an Olympic Games, a medal race in front of thousands of spectators on the inshore Nothe course. "The medal race on the Nothe course might be a bit more of a risk induced race. But it is the same for all so it shouldn't be a problem. You just have to prepare for it as best as possible. Gear choice is less important here. The medal race is 30 minutes long and it is most likely going to be in very shifty conditions, so gear will not play a big part."

For Jonas, the Olympics is all about the personal challenge. "It is the pinnacle of our sport and one of the highest challenges you can set for yourself. I like to push myself to the edge and see how far I can go. I want to win and there is no better place to do it."

"Setting short-term goals and trying to have fun with it is the key. I do miss the days where the bar in Hyeres was full of sailors halfway during the event. You don't see that any more. It's a shame. The social aspect is important. But these days, you have got to be a hard person. The ability to absorb pain and stress and come out on top is important. Being organised and not settling for second best are also elements that will help."

POSITIVE

Jonas sees the development of the class in recent years as a big positive. "I love the Finn and think it has gotten a revival with the new physical aspects. It is for sure the hardest boat on the Olympic programme. Real athletes pushing super-hard. Next time around there will be no old school sailors with a bit too much fat. They will be fit, tall and young. With that said, it looks like my time is up. So unless something radical happens it will most likely be my last Finn event."

Having spent all his Olympic career in the Finn, he has strong views on the direction the sport should take. "I think you have to identify what is interesting and what drives young people. Continuity is also important. It is hard to build a talent pool if the sport is out next time around. It becomes too risky to invest time and money. Keep it physical, get better coverage, focus on the internet."

Will he ever sail a Finn again after the Olympics? "Well, never say never, but it is unlikely. Let the young guns take over."

And finally, what was he most looking forward to as the Games approached? "Winning! Maybe too cocky, okay. Seeing the last 10 months' hard work come together with me performing my personal best, that will be the biggest satisfaction. I am truly blessed to have gotten another chance to do well at the Olympics and I will do my best to make the most of it."

EIGHT
PIETER-JAN POSTMA
INTERVIEW
'BALANCE AND CHALLENGE'

Top and middle: Pieter-Jan Postma sailed into second place at the 2011 Finn Gold Cup in Perth • Left: He also took the bronze medal at the 2011 Olympic Test Event in Weymouth

AT THE 2008 OLYMPICS PIETER-JAN POSTMA went into the event as one of the favourites. Having collected silver medals at the 2007 Finn Gold Cup and the 2007 Pre-Olympics, he looked to be at the top of his game and ready for the ultimate challenge. It didn't quite go to plan, however, and he struggled to get any consistency and failed to even make the medal race.

After that experience, he took a few years out before coming back for a second campaign. In 2011 he took the silver at the Finn Gold Cup in Perth and a bronze at the 2011 Olympic Test Event. In spite of these great results he still had to finish in the top 10 at the Finn Gold Cup in Falmouth in May to satisfy his national Federation qualification requirements.

PREPARED

He said he had learned a lot from the previous campaign and now was better prepared for what lay ahead. *"This time it was more about balance and challenge. We improved our weak points and we also improved our weapons, like starts, strategy and heavy air speed. Last time, I ran out of energy because of too much of the same and neglecting myself. I lost my motivation to race."*

He found it hard to come to terms with his performance in Qingdao. *"I started two months after the Olympics with all the wrong reasons, and after a half year without progress I took a break for a year and did another study. When I let sailing go I got a more clear view about the situation. I realised that accepting it was a weak spot in different ways, and learned to accept my negative feelings, to let them go and feel more free."*

OPPORTUNITY

But he still had a need to prove himself at the Olympics again. *"I think what I have learned is that with the things I do, it doesn't matter what I do but how I do it. That's the most important thing for me. Because I have the opportunity to do the best I can, in the sports I do now, I want to be as good as I can, sail the boat really well, get the nice shifts, to be fully in flow with the boat and the wind. What's nice is that we can work towards something and that is the Olympics. It's great to work towards that."*

"The level is high, but I don't believe the Olympics is the most important thing; it's the process that is the most important. I am really happy

I have the opportunity to do it and I have learned a lot from it as a person: to make life choices, to travel and to sail in the Olympics. The focus is the moment and the Olympics is a nice event. But the journey is more important than the moment. Everyone is looking at the Olympics, and it's fun and it's nice, but it's all about the path you take. I have become more grown-up by the whole process."

How did he get back his motivation? *"This year it's easier to get motivated but I think it's also nice to try and win a worlds. At the beginning of the four years, don't look only at the Olympics, look also at the worlds and the Europeans each year. Try to do the best you can. Make your goals challenging, but not too much. So try to always make your goals so you just reach them and get your motivation from that. Try to work with the goals. I played a lot with my goals, so you can also. Don't put the goals too far away. Keep them close and play with the level."*

PERSISTENT

"To be a great Olympian I think you have to be persistent. It takes 10 years at a high level of racing, so you need to be persistent and determined; that's the most important thing. I think some people are focusing too much on the Olympics, maybe. What Giles [Scott] did in 2011 winning the Europeans and the Gold Cup was fantastic. He was the best sailor in the world that year."

What drives you to want to do an Olympic campaign? *"It's a great learning experience. It's fantastic. Also it's nice to prove yourself and be a part of it. But you have to be hard on yourself. You have to be honest with yourself. You work on your characteristics. It's a great thing. You learn about other nationalities. It is great taking challenges and step by step to be better."*

"Sailing is quite a complex sport, so I try to let my unconscious do almost all of it; directing my conscious to take the best and objective information. So one of my main rituals is to clear my mind."

What was his gear choice for Weymouth? *"The plan was early ready. I am using a stiff HIT mast with a soft top with full sails. North for strong winds, with steady profile. WB for lighter winds for more adjustable profile."*

VISION

How does he think that Olympic sailing should move forward? *"To me it looks like the ISAF is reacting to the IOC and personal opinions on what's happening on the moment. I would like to see the ISAF together with a few experienced athletes taking charge to make an 8/40 year vision and a strategy to get there. To be ahead of IOC wishes, and still keep the pure core of the sailing sport."*

Who were his favourites for medals at the Games (again excluding himself)? *"Ben Ainslie, Jonas Høgh-Christensen, Jonathan Lobert."*

And what next? *"We now have a small Finn team with great key people; Coach Stefan de Vries, sponsor and media manager Alexandra Verbeek and material expert Jan van der Horst. This is fantastic, but I am by myself in the boat. In sailing I would like to focus more on teamwork. I would like to support and be part of a team and performing together at the highest level. I want to put all my energy in an AC or VOR campaign."*

NINE
BEN AINSLIE INTERVIEW
'HOPES OF A NATION'

AFTER WINNING SILVER IN THE Laser in 1996 and gold in 2000, Ben Ainslie moved into the Finn class and won back-to-back gold medals in 2004 and 2008. Heading into the 2012 Games Ben was on the brink of becoming the most successful Olympic sailor of all time. This accolade had been held by another Finn sailor, Paul Elvstrøm, since 1960 after winning four Olympic gold medals from 1948 to 1960, the first in a Firefly and then three in the Finn. If Ainslie won gold on Sunday 5 August, he would beat Elvstrøm's record and enter the history books yet again.

Although he was the outright favourite to take a third Finn gold, it was never going to be an easy task. At 35 he was one of the oldest sailors in the Finn fleet and sailing what was potentially his last Olympic Games. But in this highly competitive fleet he had almost completely dominated the 2011 and 2012 seasons, notching up impressive victories at the 2011 Olympic Test Event and the 2012 Finn Gold Cup, his sixth Finn World Championship.

SPECIAL

What was so special about this Olympics to him? *"Really because it's a home Olympics which makes it very special. I was in Trafalgar Square when they announced that London had won the bid for 2012. The atmosphere was electric and that's when I decided I wanted to continue my Olympic career and be a part of it."*

Ben's profile within sailing, and especially within UK sport, was at an all time high. His image had been used to publicise the London 2012 Olympic Games – probably a first for a sailor – and he carried the hopes of the whole nation to win the gold. In light of this, did he regard the 2012 Olympics as the most important regatta in his life? *"It is the most important regatta in my life right now, but they were all important to get to this point. In my mind I focus on the event and what I have to do to be successful; I can't worry about anything else."*

PREPARATION

How had his preparation differed from the 2008 campaign? *"I guess I have had more time to prepare for it and I have had to as the home competition has been tougher and the venue is also tough strategically. The international competition is very similar to what it was four years ago, although the expected conditions are very different."*

Top to bottom: Ben Ainslie at the 2011 Finn Gold Cup in Perth • The 2012 Finn Gold Cup in Falmouth • Leading the fleet into the finish of the medal race at the 2011 Olympic Test Event in Weymouth

In China Ben's coach was the former British Finn sailor Jez Fanstone, who is now Olympic manager for the New Zealand team. For Weymouth Ben had teamed up again with David 'Sid' Howlett. *"They are both very experienced. I guess Sid is slightly more so when it comes to Olympic experience, but both Sid and Jez are very professional and committed and that is what you want in a coach. I look for someone who I get on well with and who has the experience. It's also important that they share the same determination for the campaign to be successful. I should also say that I have been really fortunate to have so much help and support over the years from many different people."*

Some would say that Ben was lucky to race for a country that has such a high level of Finn sailing, with two other sailors who had won the World Championship in recent years and several others always near the top. While this had no doubt raised his game over the years, it was hard on the other sailors such as Edward Wright and Giles Scott, who suffered under the rules of one nation per class in the sailing at the Olympics. Does Ben think this is one rule that should be changed so that all the top sailors have the chance to sail? *"As an elitist I would say yes, we should have all of the top sailors, but we also have to realise sailing's role in the Olympic Family. If we start excluding emerging nations in sailing then we risk our Olympic status. It is really hard on guys like Giles Scott and Ed Wright, but that's what you sign up for and you have to live and die by the results."*

PINNACLE

"In small boats the Olympics is the pinnacle, but having said that there are some fantastic non-Olympic sailors such as Nick Craig. I'm sure if Nick had the time to train full time he could be successful in the Olympic arena, but he has other commitments and I guess that's the choice you have to make. As a professional sailor, the Olympics, America's Cup, Volvo Ocean race, Jules Verne and Vendée Globe really mean something."

After so many years campaigning a single-handed dinghy for the Olympics, does he find it a problem to keep motivating himself? *"I have always been busy trying to mix America's Cup campaigns with Olympic campaigns. It isn't easy, but it keeps you very busy and you have to focus hard on maximising the time that you have. I find that each time I come back I have a fresh approach and seem to learn more that way."*

Are the sacrifices worth the effort? *"Personally, I set a goal and I want to achieve that goal. It would be the same with anything else in life but in this instance it's the Olympics Games and in sport it doesn't get any higher than that. I guess I don't really have a normal life. I live out of a suitcase and it's very hard on family and friends. Sometimes it isn't easy and I wonder what I am doing, but at the end of the day it's my ambition and I am very lucky to have the opportunities and support that I have had along the way."*

The path to Weymouth was paved with incidents, some of which Ben would prefer to forget. Aside from the media boat incident in Perth and the operation on his back over the winter, what was the hardest part about the campaign this time around for him? *"It has probably been adapting to the physicality of the free pumping. It requires a lot of fitness and technique. It is also a benefit for the taller guys."*

As far as gear selection goes, Ben had been playing around with a Wilke-built Finn for a while in addition to campaigning his 2004/2008 gold medal-winning Devoti hull. Ben claims to have gone through about four hulls, six masts and about 150 sails in his 10 years in the class. Is there a performance advantage with the Devoti he used? *"The [Devoti] boat was very well built by Tim Tavinor and the fact that it is still going strong eight years on is testament to that. It is different to a standard boat and I guess it gives me the confidence that if I sail well then I am competitive."*

PROCESS

"But it has been a good project working with Wilke on the hulls and masts. It was good to go through the development process and work out what was reality and what the opportunities are. We are still working on the equipment and probably won't make a final call until just prior to the Games."

As with all British athletes and sailors, there was always going to be immense domestic interest from the public and the media which would only increase the pressure on the competitors. Can you prepare for that? *"I think the crowds will be an inspiration rather than a distraction. The media are always there and you have to deal with that."* What about the controversial Nothe course area? *"I think in any breeze from the east to south-west it will be fine. Outside of that wind range I hope they will race elsewhere."*

Will there be any more Finn sailing for Ben Ainslie after these Olympics? *"I honestly don't know. After the Games I will focus on the America's Cup and then see how things develop. I have loved sailing the Finn but it will depend what my objectives are."* And his thoughts on the Olympics in general? *"ISAF need to consolidate the classes. There are too many classes and there is no room for two sets of men's and women's high-performance classes. Ultimately, in time, we need to switch to more exciting classes."*

Ben wouldn't be drawn on picking favourites for the medals. *"It's such an open class, I would say any of the top 12 guys could win a medal."*

And finally, what was he most looking forward to? *"After so much preparation I just can't wait to get on with the racing."*

TEN

DAY ONE: PERFECT SCORE FOR JONAS HØGH-CHRISTENSEN AFTER GRANDSTAND OPENING

Top to bottom: Eduard Skornyakov leads
Deniss Karpak • Downwind in race one
• Jonas Høgh-Christensen excelled in
front of the crowd on the Nothe

Opposite page • Top: Ben Ainslie produced
his best ever opening day performance
• Middle: Zach Railey tacks under
Rafael Trujillo • Bottom: Alican Kaynar,
Dan Slater, Brendan Casey and Ainslie

JONAS HØGH-CHRISTENSEN GOT AWAY to a perfect start at the London 2012 Olympic Sailing Competition as he won both races on the opening day, leading both from start to finish. Ben Ainslie was second in both races and Ivan Kljakovic Gaspic was third in both races, but each of them had to fight hard for every place.

The Finns opened the sailing at the 2012 Games with a tricky and tough race on the Nothe course area, with a grandstand of 4,500 people cheering from the grassy bank beside the Nothe Fort. The 24 Finns, decked out in their Olympic coloured banners on the sails and hulls, made a very pretty picture against the stark backdrop of Portland harbour wall and the Nothe Fort.

RACE ONE

In race one Høgh-Christensen won the pin with Florian Raudaschl just above him. Ainslie started mid line and then seemed to favour the right side of the course. With the wind gradually increasing from 11-12 knots to around 16-17 knots and gusting a bit more, the 2012 Games had opened with a tough hike-out upwind followed by a physically testing free pumping downwind leg. Given the often shifty nature of the wind on the Nothe course, it was interesting to see that the fleet was almost evenly split across the course area going upwind.

Høgh-Christensen judged the first beat perfectly to lead round from Raudaschl and Ioannis Mitakis, who were both sailing in their first Olympics. He sped away downwind and was never really threatened, winning the race by a margin of around 20 seconds. Raudaschl sailed well to stay near the front, although he finally slipped to sixth on the final downwind while Mitakis hung on for fourth.

Ainslie rounded in 10th but pulled up to third at the first gate with some superb downwind sailing. He again went right on the second beat and again lost places back to sixth. He pulled back up to third on the next downwind, but Kljakovic Gaspic had found a way into second. Ainslie finally went left on the final beat and maintained his place and then moved into second on the final downwind with Kljakovic Gaspic crossing in third.

Brendan Casey had the misfortune to capsize while trying to recover from a bad first beat and in climbing back into his boat caused the hull to separate from his deck and create a large leak into the inner compartments. He retired from the race. He later said, "*We are lucky it is this length of an event and I am confident I can come back from this result.*"

RACE TWO

The second race, sailed out in Weymouth Bay in slightly less wind, though still with Oscar flag up for free pumping, followed a similar pattern, with Høgh-Christensen winning the pin again and sailing away from the fleet. He rounded the top mark with a 30-second lead over Ainslie in second. Casey rounded in third, but his makeshift repairs were not holding well and he slowed up and dropped to seventh as seawater found its way into his boat. Kljakovic Gaspic worked his way up to third on the second beat, but couldn't catch the two leaders. Høgh-Christensen held on to a 19-second lead from Ainslie, who was nearly a minute ahead of Kljakovic Gaspic at the finish. Ainslie had made inroads into Høgh-Christensen's lead downwind but just couldn't quite catch him.

While there had been a lot of talk about Ainslie's chance to become the greatest sailing Olympian of all time - if he won gold this week he would break the record held by Paul Elvstrøm - today people also started talking about Høgh-Christensen protecting that record for Denmark. Both sailors stated that such records were not their most immediate concerns. Høgh-Christensen said, "*That was not my main focus. Paul Elvstrøm was the greatest sailor of all time. If I get a chance to protect that legacy, that's what I will do. I hope I can protect that legacy.*"

Of course, it was worth remembering that the four time Olympic medalist Ainslie had just sailed his best opening day ever - by a long way – at an Olympic Games. At previous Games he had always picked up high scores or suffered some misfortune.

Ainslie said, "*It wasn't the greatest of races in the beginning, but that spurred me on. I have been better, but it is where you finish.*" The crowd on the Nothe provided encouragement. "*I could hear it clearly and it really spurred me on.*" On Høgh-Christensen's performance he said, "*I think he is doing the best he can for himself right now.*"

Høgh-Christensen added, "*It was a good day. I got the shifts right on the Nothe course. Great crowd, great experience. I felt like a football player walking into a stadium. Hearing the crowd was an excellent high. We did a lot of good preparation and I felt good and confident going into the regatta.*" And looking forwards? "*Keep cool. Take it one day at a time and keep focused.*"

Kljakovic Gaspic said, "*It was a good day. I didn't have perfect starts but I was pushing hard and it paid off in the end. Two third places makes me happy and relaxed for following days. Jonas sailed a great day, with clear starts and great speed, and that made him unbeatable on the water today.*"

The 2008 silver medalist Zach Railey didn't have the opening day that he had hoped for, with a 10th and a 15th to sit in 15th overall. "*We are fine as far as boat speed is concerned, but I made an error on the first beat in the second race and was pretty far behind with no real chances to get back to front group. But we will be ready for tomorrow. There's still a long way to go.*"

ELEVEN

DAY TWO: HØGH-CHRISTENSEN EXTENDS AFTER DAY OF DRAMA

Top to bottom: Dan Slater, winner of race three • Start of race two • Zach Railey wins the pin end at the start

ON DAY TWO IN WEYMOUTH the man of the moment, Jonas Høgh-Christensen, extended his lead and, while Jonathan Lobert moved up to second, there was a four-way tie for third place. Race wins went to the Dan Slater and Daniel Birgmark.

It was another windy and beautiful day in Weymouth with sunny skies and 14-16 knots of breeze in the morning. The Finns sailed two great races on the Weymouth Bay West course and there was plenty of drama to keep the viewers happy.

RACE THREE

Race three belonged to Slater. After having to wait a long time to have his national selection for these Games confirmed, he proved his ability with a stunning performance in testing conditions to dominate and win race three by nearly 30 seconds. He rounded the top mark with a narrow lead from Pieter-Jan Postma and Ioannis Mitakis and extended on every leg.

By the bottom mark Mitakis had dropped down the fleet while overall leader Høgh-Christensen had climbed to second, with Postma in third. Ben Ainslie climbed up to fourth on the run but lost places upwind again and finally finished in sixth. The top three remained the same, with Slater extending to win by half a minute. Third overall Ivan Kljakovic Gaspic recovered from 14th at the top mark to seventh at the finish.

RACE FOUR

The fourth race was full of drama. First Høgh-Christensen hit the pin end on the start and after rerounding headed out right to clear his wind, but in last place. Ainslie also had a bad start and at the top mark the two regatta leaders were 14th and 21st. At the front Tapio Nirkko rounded first from Birgmark and Rafael Trujillo. Nirkko then capsized at the downwind mark, but recovered his boat quickly and rejoined the race in sixth.

Then Trujillo also capsized after his rudder popped off. The new leader was Jonathan Lobert, who had moved up to second on the downwind. Lobert held onto the lead round the next windward mark but the fleet had compressed slightly, with Høgh-Christensen making the biggest gain to round in seventh.

He had taken more than a minute out of his deficit on the first leg to trail the new leader by just 30 seconds. Ainslie had dropped to 12th, another 30 seconds back. Two offwind legs remained to the finish and it was a great test of stamina and strength as well as a thrilling finish.

With the wind increasing to 18-19 knots, Birgmark powered down the run and just sneaked round the leeward mark ahead of Lobert to scream down the final reach and take the winner's gun. Lobert crossed three seconds later with Vasilij Zbogar another two seconds after that in third. While Kljakovic Gaspic moved from 13th to ninth, neither Høgh-Christensen nor Ainslie could make any gains.

However, a seventh for Høgh-Christensen was easily enough to retain the overall lead by eight points from Lobert, with Ainslie, Kljakovic Gaspic, Postma and Zbogar all on equal points, three points further back.

Nirkko said of his brief spell at the front, "*Finally I got some of the big lines right and had good speed and rounded in the lead. I stretched out a bit until the downwind mark. I was hassling with the sheet and it slipped out of my hands and the boom went all the way out and – I think it was a combination of the position of the boat on the wave and heeling of the boat – I capsized to windward.*"

"*Fortunately I had such a comfortable lead before that, so when I got the boat up and started to sail again, the leaders were not too far away. I guess after a capsize a fifth place is all right. I just have to think about the points rather than the feeling it created.*"

On his regatta so far, "*Generally not really very good, but leading today gave me some confidence that I could be at the top. And after four races I am quite consistent, so I've not had any bombs in the series, so that's a good thing.*"

Birgmark, the race four winner, said, "*It was not as shifty as yesterday. In the second race I got the shifts right, which I didn't in the first when I went right early on and a big left shift came and I was almost last. It was too much distance to catch up. But I am very happy with my last downwind when I managed to pass Jonathan. He rounded the top mark just ahead and I was just in front at the downwind mark.*"

"*It was tough on the last reach to the finish but I had it under control. But the downwind was really interesting to just be in front for the mark rounding. It's a shame, though, that Tapio capsized while in the lead.*"

HØGH-CHRISTENSEN

Leader after four races, Høgh-Christensen said, "*I am very happy so far. Today was actually a good day.*"

"*In the first race I didn't know what was going to happen with the wind. There was big cloud coming down the race course and I thought it could go both ways so I decided to start in the middle and play it safe. I didn't get the greatest start, but I played it safe and played the middle up the beat and rounded the windward mark in sixth or seventh. And then I had a good downwind and got to second. So that was good.*"

"*Then in the second race I hit the pin end committee boat. It was really frustrating and a stupid, stupid mistake. It was a little bit of tide and a bit of bad timing. I had a chance to bail out at 20 seconds but didn't take it when I should have. I had to go round and do a turn and started way last and had to fight my way back up. I fought my way back to the top guys and was right next to them downwind and then passed them on the second beat so I was really happy with that. It was fantastic to come back like that, but I pushed really, really hard and it felt good.*"

On fitness, "*I am probably not the strongest guy out there but strong enough; and luckily I have been in a couple of races where I have been far enough ahead to take it easy and save my energy for the next race.*"

On the forecast for moderate to strong breeze for the rest of the week, "*I think it shows off our sport in the best possible way and makes it interesting sailing and good fun to watch. So it couldn't be much better.*"

On the surprisingly poor results from the favourite, Ainslie. "*I don't think it's the wind. Ben dominated the worlds in Falmouth not more than three months ago in this much wind and more. Since then people have upped their game and I think sometimes you can have a good week and sometimes you don't; but as I said earlier, knowing Ben, he'll be fired up tomorrow and he'll come back like thunder, so let's see what happens. He usually gets fired up when things aren't going well.*"

Ainslie was in agreement with this. "*I wasn't happy with my own performance. It will get me fired up for the rest of the week. It's a very fine line between success and failure at this level. I don't think I went the right way all day. Hopefully it will go a lot better.*"

TWELVE
DAY THREE: CLEAR LEAD FOR GREAT DANE AT HALF WAY STAGE

Top and bottom: Despite showing great form at times, Rafael Trujillo suffered from a series of unlucky gear failures during the week • Middle: Downwind in race three – Piotr Kula and Brendan Casey

JONAS HØGH-CHRISTENSEN AGAIN EXTENDED on the fleet with a first and second on day three. Ben Ainslie moved up to second after a better day, but still had yet to beat the Great Dane after six races. Jonathan Lobert dropped one place to third. The second race of the day was won by Deniss Karpak.

Tuesday was crunch day for the Finns. Going into the halfway stage of the regatta, Ainslie needed to make some points back before the lay day on Wednesday, while regatta leader Høgh-Christensen was looking to consolidate his points lead and not do anything silly.

RACE FIVE

Race five was dominated by Høgh-Christensen from start to finish. Starting in the pack, but away from the pin-end boat he had hit the day before, he soon pulled ahead of the fleet and, with Postma suffering gear failure on the far left, the Dane steered a confident course up the favoured left side of the course to round the top mark with a small lead over Rafael Trujillo, Ainslie and Zach Railey, while several boats overstood in the strong tide. Ainslie had started in the middle and was soon in difficulty, having to tack away to clear his air.

After a screaming reach towards the wing mark as the wind piped up, there was a fascinating duel between the leading bunch on the run, although Høgh-Christensen started to pull away from the fleet. Railey, the 2008 silver medalist, hadn't had a great regatta thus far, so was also looking for improvements. He had moved up to second at the gate, sailing past the normally faster Ainslie. Ainslie rounded behind and had to tack away to find a lane further to the right. Høgh-Christensen seemed confident on the left and held his course before coming back with a nice lead into the second top mark.

The wind faded on the final offwind legs, but Høgh-Christensen extended his lead, while Railey maintained second from Trujillo. While Nirkko and Ainslie passed Trujillo, Ainslie also looked to be closing on Nirkko but ran out of track. At the finish it was Høgh-Christensen, Railey, Nirkko and Ainslie, with Ivan Kljakovic Gaspic staging an amazing recovery from 19th at the first mark to cross fifth.

RACE SIX

Ainslie was now firmly on the back foot and needed something special in race six. He started well, winning the pin after Postma returned and controlled the lane to the favoured left side of the course and looked to be coming into the top mark well placed.

Meanwhile, Høgh-Christensen was forced to tack off to find clear air and trailed on the right. However, many boats overstood the top mark and first round was Trujillo from Ioannis Mitakis, Nirkko and Høgh-Christensen. Ainslie finally rounded in seventh.

Trujillo led down the run with Deniss Karpak moving up to second ahead of Nirkko and Ainslie. By the gate Karpak had made big gains to round in first from Nirkko, Ainslie and Høgh-Christensen. The Dane was forced to tack away again after he had been passed by Ainslie for the first time all week. It was all change on the final upwind however, with Høgh-Christensen splitting from the fleet and making places all the way up to second to round behind Karpak. Trujillo rounded third from Vasilij Zbogar while Ainslie slipped to fifth.

Karpak extended down the run to lead into the finish and win by nearly a minute. Høgh-Christensen rounded in second, but Ainslie had caught up for a thrilling spray-filled chase to the line. It was a tight finish, but the Dane just held on for second with Ainslie third, Trujillo fourth and Zbogar fifth.

LOBERT

Despite dropping one place to third, Lobert said, *"I am pretty happy so far. Third overall after three days means I am still in the game. We still have four races to go and so I will take it day by day, race by race, like I have done since the beginning. And I always try my hardest to catch up the most boats I can when I am behind. Today I was 15th and 17th at the first mark, which is not so good."* Lobert recovered to place sixth and seventh.

"The racing is very tight. The wind today was a bit strange, very up and down and sometimes there was some oil on the water. On the first upwinds I didn't know exactly what to do. I was just looking around and missed most of the shifts. Then slowly, slowly I came back during the race and so I am pretty happy with that."

"I want to improve my first upwind. If I can be top six round the first mark I have a good chance to win the race, like I almost did yesterday. I maybe have to take more risks on the start line. In the first race today the Greek was just above me and he was OCS. I thought we were pretty high but I held back. But I also need to improve my tactics. I need to have a better plan for the first upwind, as most of the time I don't have a plan and am not sure what to do. I just try for the start and then react to where I am, which is not so good."

Postma described his unfortunate gear failure. *"The wind was left and you had to be left and win the pin end. I was going a bit low, going for speed and I wanted to tighten the outhaul a bit more so I pulled it with some force and broke it. I took down the sail, fixed it, but then the fleet was gone."*

"I was calm at the time. These things happen. Then I felt a bit disappointed, then a bit angry. Now I just feel focused. We have a rest day to gain all the energy back and I am looking forward to getting on with the racing."

The 2008 silver medalist Railey had enjoyed his best day so far with a 2, 8 to rise to 12th overall. He said, *"Today was better. I did nothing different but just had the shifts go the way I thought. It's been hard to get the wind correct, but I am still fighting hard. I just need to have good races. I am in quite a hole from the first few races, but I will not quit. Looking forward to a day off to watch some other races on TV and recover my legs."*

Høgh-Christensen said, *"In both races I wanted to go left. So starting close to the pin was the plan, but with a bit less risk. Both starts were good, but I thought I was over in the second race and went back. The reason being that I was on the line with PJ and he went back. Apparently none of us were over. I came back fast and managed to hit some good shifts to get back to fourth. Then I gained a couple more and I am super-content with that. Another good day."*

"You have got to take your breaks when you can. I am an old man in the fleet and I definitely need a rest, a big steak and ready up for Thursday."

AINSLIE

Ainslie commented on his performance, *"It's tough. Sometimes these things work out, but unfortunately for me this week it hasn't. I was really frustrated yesterday, but it has been better today."*

"He [Høgh-Christensen] is sailing really well. He is a good sailor and a big guy. He is having the regatta of his life. He likes upwind and for whatever reason he is nailing it every time. If I keep pushing hard he might slip up. It's a difficult place to sail here, but he keeps nailing it. He is sailing well and at some point the tables have to turn. He's on fire."

After three days' tough racing the fleet now had a rest day - and a day to think about how they would approach the final four opening series races on Thursday and Friday. While one man would be trying to relax and keep his head clear, another would be evaluating what had gone so wrong. Ainslie may have been in the silver medal position, but he had openly admitted that anything other than gold would be a disaster. And after six races he was sitting 10 points behind the Dane with a little bomb on his scorecard (a 12th) waiting to be ignited if he had another bad day.

Høgh-Christensen was producing the type of performance that everyone expected Ainslie to produce. Some great race wins, all-round speed dominance and some incredible comebacks. What did Ainslie have to do to turn this around? And did he know the answer himself? How do you respond to someone sailing the way Høgh-Christensen had done? This was an unusual situation for Ainslie, as normally it was the rest of the fleet working out how to respond to Ainslie's dominance. It was going to be fascinating to watch it play out.

THIRTEEN
LAY DAY: FINNS PREPARE FOR FINAL PUSH ON WEYMOUTH'S WATERS

Top to bottom: Florian Raudaschl had a great first race on the flatter waters on the Nothe course but struggled on the offshore courses • Jorge Zarif was the youngest Finn sailor in Weymouth but was gaining valuable experience for 2016 • Tapio Nirkko was having a few good races but still sitting in the top 10 overall

JUST THREE WEEKS PREVIOUSLY JONAS Høgh-Christensen had said in an interview, *"..we did push the bar and I can say we found some magic on the way. What it is will show at the Games."*

How true those words had become. He had created the big story of the sailing events to date, grabbing headline news across the UK and the world while he humbled the three-time Olympic champion Ben Ainslie. In the first six races Ainslie had yet to beat the newly tagged 'Great Dane'. Wednesday was a day off and while most of the sailors rested and rebuilt their energy, Ainslie was working out how he would approach the final four races of the opening series to overcome his Danish nemesis.

Apart from the hint of prescience in Christensen's words, nobody would ever have believed that Ainslie would be so far behind at the halfway stage in the regatta. The next four races would set the scene for Sunday's medal race and on the form so far it was quite conceivable that the gold would be nearly settled by then.

However, Ainslie is never more dangerous than when he is down. He had proved that time and time again over the years. They say, never make him angry, you won't like him when he's angry. He was really angry after Monday's showing of a sixth and a 12th, but his response on Tuesday, of a fourth and a third, and both behind Høgh-Christensen, was not exactly the kind of response that everyone expected – and definitely not the response that would drag him back into contention.

Thursday's races would therefore be crucial to see whether he possessed the arsenal to respond in a useful way. He didn't just need to start beating the Dane; he needed to put boats between them as well to reduce the points deficit. While early weather predictions forecast lighter conditions – which would have played in Ainslie's favour - later it looked as though it would be just as windy as the races so far and maybe more so. Questions had already been asked about Ainslie's fitness and his gear selection, but he knew the only way to answer that was on the water.

POSTMA

Sixth overall Pieter-Jan Postma spent his day off with his family and was optimistic about his chances, despite suffering several setbacks so far. He was in sixth place and 12 points outside the medals. He said, *"I feel good. The first day I was a little bit tense. I have had to play some catch-up a few times and I missed a few shifts. But I am looking forward to five more races. It's a nice fight. I really like the Games."*

"It's great to see Jonas sailing so well. This is really good. And I hope he keeps on doing it like this. He's the best sailor here. Jonas sails better, he sails consistently, has good speed, is smart on the downwind. He always does the right thing."

Jonathan Lobert was in the bronze medal position, one down from his silver at the test event. *"I was expecting to be a little bit more nervous actually, but I have been having a lot of fun and I am just seeing it as a normal regatta, so I'll just do my job as always."* On his day off, *"I will relax in Weymouth, maybe find a good place to eat. No sailing or training. Just relax and build energy for the coming days."*

Greg Douglas was in 15th place and 32 points off the medal race, which was his goal. This was his second Olympics after sailing the Laser in 2008. *"It's hard and it's tough. The level is just so high. We're fighting for inches and millimetres out there. The racing has been great, though, with great waves and wind. It's been perfect, everything you could ask for."*

How did he get into Finns? *"I had outgrown the Laser and I was struggling to keep my weight under 190 lb. I stopped racing Lasers and started coaching in 2008. I first stepped in a Finn in 2009. Chris Cook invited myself, Brendan Wilton and Paul Brikis to try out the Finn and since then I haven't looked back. My first event was at the Miami OCR in 2010."*

Douglas famously beat his coach, Cook, in the Canadian trials after Cook took ill, but he said, *"The trials were very tough and I would like to thank Chris for everything he has done for me."*

"I know I can do a lot better than I am doing so I am not that happy with my performance so far. It has been a bit of a one-way track at times with the left paying. But getting a lane to go left has been tough. And then my downwind speed hasn't been as great as it normally is so that's been tough. I've been in the fight, but I think there are a few races where I could have been a few places higher. But the experience has been great. Being at the Olympics is always fun and I'm learning so much for next time. There will be a lot more to come from me."

RAUDASCHL

A bit further down the field was Florian , one of the older sailors in the fleet, but at his first Olympics. He was in 20th place, though he showed some clear potential by briefly leading race one. *"I am completely tired. It's not my conditions. Too windy, too big waves. First day was OK with flat water and that's what I prefer and I am just waiting for light winds, but it never seems to happen in Weymouth."*

He has been sailing the Finn since 1999. *"No sailing before that, only a lot of windsurfing. So no Optimist or Laser time for me. The main reason was that there was not enough wind on our lakes for windsurfing. So I jumped into a Finn for fun and immediately liked it. When my father heard this, he bought me a Finn and that was my start."* His father is, of course, Hubert Raudaschl, silver medalist in the Finn in 1968. In Austria, *"The newspapers like the 'father and son' story, so there is quite some interest there. The fact that there is no snow on the ski slopes right now and the Austrian soccer teams are bad helps to get some interest in sailing. As nearly none of my friends are sailing at home, even they show some interest now – which feels a bit strange."*

On the remaining races, *"It's tough. I think I am just too small in these conditions. But I am really enjoying the experience. That's perfect. It is also very interesting to see the battle at the front. It's really exciting to watch Ben and Jonas and the other guys fight it out. Jonas is so fast at the moment. Upwind he is unbelievable, but still five races to go so we'll see what happens."*

Ioannis Mitakis started the year on a high, winning the light wind Europeans, but he has struggled so far and was in 13th place, but just 10 points off the medal race. He joined the class in 2009 after becoming too big for the Laser but made fast progress, winning two European junior titles before taking the senior title earlier in 2012. His strength is upwind and several times during the week he had rounded in the front bunch. Unfortunately, one of those was an OCS.

He had struggled to get much regatta time since then. *"Due to the economic problems that my country faces, all athletes have to cut expenses. So my budget was enough to sail the Europeans, Sail for Gold and one training camp in Weymouth. The only thing you need to train is water and wind and we have plenty of those in Greece. I came to the venue three times, first time in Pre-Olympics then Sail for Gold 2012 and finally a training camp before the Olympics. The main thing I have learned is that sometimes the local knowledge of the current is more important than wind shifts."*

However, he was upbeat about his performance. *"I think it's going pretty well so far. Yesterday I had a bad start with an OCS, but otherwise so far it is going OK. I am happy with my speed upwind, though I am losing places on the downwind."*

ZARIF

Finn sailing was in the family for Jorge Zarif. His late father competed in the Finn in the 1984 and 1988 Olympics. *"I feel happy to be here because it is something that would make him proud of me. All the work I have done over the last 15 years is paying off, so it's an honour for me and my family to sail in the Olympics."* Zarif, who was junior Finn world champion in 2009, was the youngest Finn sailor in Weymouth at just 19. *"In September 2006 I was a Laser sailor and my father had a Finn. There was a race in Sao Paulo, my home town, and he was injured and asked if I wanted to go in his boat. I said yes."*

Zarif was lying in 19th place, with a lot of work to do to make the medal race. His real goal, however, is his home Olympics in Rio in 2016 and he is treating this year as a learning exercise. *"I want finish top 10. It's hard but possible. But it's also a good experience for the next Olympics."*

FOURTEEN
DAY FOUR: AINSLIE STRIKES BACK BUT HØGH-CHRISTENSEN STILL LEADS

Top to bottom: Ivan Kljakovic Gaspic was always pushing the leaders but was picking up too many points • The crucial start of race seven and Ben Ainslie wins the pin to dominate for his first win of the week • Ainslie leads Rafael Trujillo and Pieter-Jan Postma

BEN AINSLIE RETURNED TO WINNING ways on day four with a first and a third to narrow the gap on regatta leader Jonas Høgh-Christensen to just three points. Ivan Kljakovic Gaspic moved back up to third, while the second race of the day was won by Rafael Trujillo.

It was a big day out on Weymouth Bay course with big winds, big waves and bigger stakes. For Ainslie it was crucial that he started to narrow the points gap and he did just that. Today was the day that he had to make his move on Høgh-Christensen before it was too late. The Brit was fast running out of races to reverse the points difference and he came out looking more confident and dominant that at any time so far.

RACE SEVEN

Ainslie owned the start of race seven, locking into the dangerous pin end position early and controlling it with perfection until the gun. The Dane was just to windward and just a bit back from the line, but his problem was the Polish boat that was ahead and on his wind. Piotr Kula was OCS, but he damaged Høgh-Christensen's start enough so that he had to tack to get clear air.

Ainslie controlled the left along with Trujillo and Pieter-Jan Postma and they rounded the first mark in this order with Vasilij Zbogar in fourth and then Høgh-Christensen. With big winds and big waves, the reach to the wing was a spray-filled sleigh ride. The Dane slid into fourth and then after rounding the mark dived low to get some separation from the leading bunch. Then disaster struck as he capsized on a big wave. He was up and sailing again in 30 seconds, but looked clearly rattled as he rejoined the race in 15th.

At the front Ainslie and Postma were battling for supremacy downwind in the big conditions, rounding opposite gates. Postma briefly got in front of Ainslie at the next top mark, but Ainslie soon passed him downwind to extend and win his first race of the week. He crossed the line some 20 seconds ahead of Postma, with Kljakovic Gaspic third and Tapio Nirkko fourth. Third overall Jonathan Lobert was fifth. Høgh-Christensen had climbed back to sixth at the top mark but dropped two on the downwind to cross in eighth. Early performer Trujillo again had gear problems downwind and dropped to 15th at the finish.

The British supporters breathed a collective sign of relief. Ainslie had turned the corner and had finally put a bullet on the scoreboard. More importantly for Ainslie, Høgh-Christensen now had to count his seventh from Monday, so the points gap was down to just four.

RACE EIGHT

On to race eight and Høgh-Christensen was back on the offensive, winning the favoured pin end of the line, although he had Trujillo just to windward of him. Ainslie started slightly further up the line but was soon forced to tack off to find a lane. The fleet again favoured the left, with Ainslie heading furthest left when the leaders crossed back.

Round the top mark Trujillo led from Høgh-Christensen, Postma, Nirkko and Ainslie. The Brit went low on the reach and moved up to fourth and then overtook Postma on the run. At the gate the top four boats rounded the same mark within 10 seconds of each other with a nice gap on the fleet. Just after rounding the gate for the final upwind there was high drama as Ainslie did a penalty turn and lost ground. Both Postma and Høgh-Christensen claimed he had touched the mark. Ainslie furiously denied it but did his turn anyway. Høgh-Christensen then took a hitch to the right and tacked on Ainslie's wind. Again the fleet went all the way to the port layline. Trujillo held onto his lead to round ahead, with Høgh-Christensen and Postma holding a small lead over Ainslie.

The final downwind to the finish was a thrilling battle. Høgh-Christensen immediately made inroads into Trujillo's lead, while Ainslie tried to find a route past Postma so he could attack the Dane. But it was Postma who made the first move, going wide and then crossing back in front of Høgh-Christensen and Ainslie.

Round the final mark it was Trujillo leading from Postma with Ainslie just sliding round the mark ahead of Høgh-Christensen. Nothing else changed by the finish and Trujillo took the gun. Ainslie had taken around 70 metres about out of Høgh-Christensen on the run to inflict his second victory over him in one day and further close the points gap.

ARGUMENT

The argument over the mark rounding carried on ashore. Ainslie let off steam in front of the press while Postma and Høgh-Christensen told their side of the story very matter-of-factly. A clearly angry Ainslie claimed the two had teamed up against him saying, *"I had no choice and didn't want a protest."* Høgh-Christensen responded saying, *"That's a hard allegation. If two guys see somebody hit the mark then he probably hit the mark."* At the end of the day the press had a lot of good quotes from all three of them. Ainslie famously stated, *"They have made me angry – and you don't want to make me angry."*

After a third and seventh, Kljakovic Gaspic moved into bronze position. *"It was a hard day, windy but a simple race, keeping left was important. For me it wasn't easy, but I raced hard and in the end I am happy. Tomorrow it will be all about keeping the game simple, sailing fast and pushing hard."*

Lobert, now down one place in fourth, said, *"It was a rough day. There was a lot of tension this morning. I was quite nervous. I was trying to manage it and in the first race I succeeded because I had some good downwinds and managed to finish fifth. In the second I had a terrible start and then it was just too hard to come back. So not so good a day for me."*

Postma had his best day yet with two second places. *"The wind was quite up and down. Especially on the downwinds you had to really look. In the first race I had a good start, sailed to the left side and it was a steady race. I had a fight with Ben. I passed him on the second upwind and he passed me on the last run on a gust. In the second race I had a bad start but on the upwind I caught a nice gust when I was more to the left and caught up a lot. Then I caught up to second on the reach and had a good downwind. Tomorrow I want to do better than today. I haven't showed everything I have yet. I don't feel nervous now, but tomorrow I might feel a bit nervous and I think that's fine."*

Dan Slater was still in with a slight chance at a medal, sitting in eighth place. *"It was not a very good day for me today. I had an all right first one but not a very good second one. It was just frustrating. We are sailing in three knots of current and a washing machine of waves so it's tough. It's a one-way track. But I'm still alive. They've done a fantastic job here. The facilities on shore and everything are just great. And the starts and race management have been fantastic."*

A fourth and a fifth put Nirkko in seventh place just 14 points off the medals. *"In the first race I didn't get a very good start, so I had to tack away behind the whole fleet, so I was on the wrong side and struggled on the first upwind. After that I eased the clutch and just let it go. The reach and the first downwind were good. Nothing much happened on the second upwind, but the second downwind was excellent. I think I got better pressure and was a bit more on the inside."* Nirkko went from 11th to fourth on the run after rounding the top mark in 21st.

Høgh-Christensen's lead had dropped from 10 points to just three, but he remained optimistic. *"I wanted to go left and I had a good lane but I had to tack off because of the Polish boat and that ruined the first beat for me. Then in one moment of not being on top of the boat, I flipped to windward. It was one of the expensive ones. In the second race I got the start I wanted and had a good lane. I didn't sail a good second run and lost PJ and Ben. Ben sat on me quite a lot so there were times when I didn't have much pressure."* Was it nerves? *"I don't think I was more nervous this morning that any other day. But you're always a bit nervous at the Olympics. We have a very detailed plan from when we wake up to when we go to bed and we've been following that plan and it seems to work and it takes a lot of the pressure off."*

There was just one more day of the opening series to sail before the medal race. Today was proof, if needed, that it would be a fight all the way to the finish. Ainslie was more aggressive, faster upwind, made fewer mistakes and was blisteringly fast downwind. He seemed to have overcome the lacklustre performance of the first three days and refocused on the job in hand. Høgh-Christensen, by contrast, made several mistakes and the capsize in race seven would hang over him in the days that remained. This dramatic change in fortunes had set up a thrilling match between these two amazing sailors.

FIFTEEN
DAY FIVE: AND THEN THERE WERE THREE

JONAS HØGH-CHRISTENSEN HAD LED the regatta from the very first mark. After losing just one point to defending Olympic champion, Ben Ainslie, on the final day of the opening series, the Dane would go into the medal race on Sunday 5 August with just a two-point lead. The best showing on Friday had come from Pieter-Jan Postma, who moved up to bronze position. The gold medal would come from one of these sailors. It was down to just three.

In practice this meant that whoever out of Høgh-Christensen and Ainslie finished ahead of the other would win the gold medal, providing they were in the top seven boats. Postma could mathematically win gold but needed to put at least six boats between himself and both the others. Realistically that was unlikely to happen, so the gold was now expected to be decided between the Dane and the Brit.

RACE NINE

With tempers and egos bubbling over, the Finn fleet set out for the final day of the opening series. Høgh-Christensen held a scant three-point lead over Ainslie. After a difference of opinion between them the day before, everyone expected fireworks on the water, but it didn't quite turn out that way.

Of the two of them, the Dane made the better start in race nine and, with the fleet heading to the left yet again, the pin end was bunched up. Høgh-Christensen did well on the left, forcing Ainslie to tack off, while Postma did well on the right. As they approached the top mark Ainslie had trouble finding a clean lane and trailed round in ninth. Ioannis Mitakis led round from Postma, Brendan Casey and then Høgh-Christensen.

By the gate, Postma had worked out a 50 metre lead and he extended away to comfortably win his first race of the series. Behind him there was a tense battle, with bronze medal positioned Ivan Kljakovic Gaspic making a huge gain on the downwind to move from 19th to fifth at the gate. Jonathan Lobert also gained to second, with Vasilij Zbogar close behind in third.

On the final beat Postma pulled further away while Zbogar found his way into second. Nothing much else changed in the closing stages except that Kljakovic Gaspic moved into fourth from Christensen while Ainslie took three places on the final downwind to finish one place behind the Dane.

The net result of this was that Høgh-Christensen had extended his lead by one crucial point on Ainslie. Kljakovic Gaspic was still in the bronze medal position but the points were now really tight. The last opening series race was going to be crucial for all of them. There was also the not-so-small matter of making the cut for the medal race and some sailors were looking rather precarious.

Top to bottom: Start of race 10 • Ben Ainslie had narrowed the gap to the top to just two points by the end of day five • Denmark's Jonas Høgh-Christensen would lead the fleet into the medal race

RACE TEN

For the final opening series race Postma and Ainslie started well by the pin while Høgh-Christensen was forced to tack away. Postma went furthest left and came back just above Ainslie, while Høgh-Christensen was struggling out to the right. As they approached the top mark it was clear that the left was still paying and Postma rounded first from Ainslie, Greg Douglas, Mitakis, Rafael Trujillo and Høgh-Christensen.

While Ainslie soon passed Postma and just sailed away from the fleet, Høgh-Christensen put on a surge to pass four boats and round the gate in second, but nearly a minute behind Ainslie. On the second beat, Ainslie slowed up for a while and looked to be waiting for the Dane. He would have liked to have one boat between then to make life easier in the medal race. But Postma found a way past Høgh-Christensen and Ainslie carried on. Ainslie finally rounded the top mark with a 90 metre lead and led down to the finish.

Postma was not about to make the same mistake twice and held onto his second place, while Trujillo briefly threatened Høgh-Christensen on the final run. The single point gained and lost here was just as important to Postma as it was to Høgh-Christensen.

At the finish Ainslie led by a considerable margin while Postma held on to second. Høgh-Christensen had to settle for third with Trujillo fourth. Casey sailed his best race of the series with a fifth, but it was too late to make the medal race. However, Trujillo's fourth place was enough to make the cut, relegating Deniss Karpak to 11th.

TRUJILLO

Trujillo must have been the unluckiest person in Weymouth. Over the course of the week he had suffered numerous random gear failings. His mainsheet, halyard, rudder and kicking strap had all failed at key moments causing him to lose all hope of a second medal to add to the silver he had won in 2004 in Athens. *"Making the medal race is not really any consolation for all that has happened this week after all the work we have done in the past years. But three top 10s in three consecutive Games is not a bad result. We have checked everything 100 times before the Games. I have never lost a rudder upwind before."*

"But if it's not meant to be then it's not meant to be. I would say that this is the best venue we have ever had for an Olympic Games. Also the level of the class is higher than ever. And the medal race is going to be really interesting. There will be a battle for the gold, for the bronze and for seventh as no-one will want to be last. I will try my hardest and try to end the week on a high point, despite what has happened to me."

Lobert said, *"I think a lot can happen in the medal race. It's pretty tight actually, just five points, so I can do it. And the other good point is that all the guys in the medal race can win it. So everybody will try to play their games. I think I have an advantage on the short course. Usually I am pretty good in the medal race. I kind of like them. It's very intense and short, so we'll see. I think Ben will try to put the pressure on Jonas but he has to take care as well with PJ. So Ben has to put Jonas behind him but he also has to do a good race. That's why it's pretty open, I think. It's going to be very exciting."*

"I have had a good week so tomorrow I will relax, enjoy the Games and watch the other competitions so that I am in good shape for Sunday."

After closing the gap with the leader to just two points, Ainslie said, *"I was pretty frustrated yesterday, but when you get out there you have to put it behind you and sail smart. It's taken me all week to find the turbo button and get out in front. It's good to get some more points up and even things up. The overall points were very close, so it was important for me that the Dutch sailor overtook the Dane, and finally he got past. The last two days have been huge, to draw back those points."*

TOUGH DAY

Høgh-Christensen added, *"It was a tough day today but I thought I did quite well. I didn't have the best downwind in the first race but I managed to get a fifth. I had a good pin end start and after a couple of minutes I could tack up and tack on Ben and send him out the right when he wanted to go left. I managed to pack Ben down the fleet into the teens. But we rounded the top mark in no pressure and they rounded in lots of pressure right behind us and he caught up to finish sixth."*

"In the second race I didn't get a great start but managed to fight my way back to second, but unfortunately I lost PJ on the second beat. But that's what happens. PJ is sailing fast."

On the tactical move by Ainslie on the final beat, *"Ben stopped for a bit but didn't do anything. I think he was thinking about doing something but it was probably too big a risk for him to try and put boats in between us. It was too close. He would have to had come so close that when we rounded the windward mark I would have an opportunity to pass him down the run. So I think he bailed on his plan. He got a little lucky that PJ got in front of me so now it's who beats who in the medal race."*

So, into the medal race on Sunday. Høgh-Christensen would lead Ainslie by two points while Ainslie led Postma by 14 points. Crucially, the top two had a 21 point and 19 point lead over Lobert and Kljakovic Gaspic, which meant they were all but assured a medal; just the colour needed to be decided. Postma meanwhile had a five-point lead over Lobert and Kljakovic Gaspic, with Zbogar just two points behind. The medals would all come from these six sailors.

SIXTEEN
THE BEN AND JONAS SHOW

IT HAD BEEN BUILDING ALL week long and had gone right down to the wire. The on-the-water – and sometimes off-the-water – battle between Jonas Høgh-Christensen and Ben Ainslie would reach its exciting conclusion on Sunday 5 August when the Finn class medal race at the London 2012 Olympic Sailing Competition took place.

The final showdown between Høgh-Christensen, the double world champion at his third Olympics, and Ainslie, the three-time Olympic champion and six-time Finn world champion, had ignited the interest of the worldwide press as they slavered over the prospect of the most momentous dinghy race in history.

There was a lot at stake. Ainslie was hunting for his fourth consecutive Olympic gold medal to become the most decorated Olympic sailor of all time, surpassing the original Great Dane Paul Elvstrøm's four gold medals between 1948 and 1960. There was also a slight sense that Høgh-Christensen was defending Elvstrøm's record and honour. Both were already all but guaranteed medals; the medal race would decide the colour.

PACE SETTER

Høgh-Christensen was the early pace-setter when the Finn racing started on Sunday 29 August, winning the first three races to the backdrop of a shocked British audience concerned that their golden boy, Ainslie, perhaps wasn't up to the job. Høgh-Christensen led the competition from the first mark of the first race and led going into the medal race. A lot of questions were asked of Ainslie as to what was going on, but he didn't have the answer in the first half of the week. His answer finally came on both of the two final days of the opening series as he clawed back his points deficit and showed some of his true form to go into the medal race effectively level with the Great Dane Mk 2.

During the halfway stage lay day, something changed in Ainslie. He came back out with gritted teeth, looking determined to stop the downward spiral. It still wasn't easy, however, fighting his way back twice from lowly positions at the top mark. But that is what had made him famous – making incredible comebacks against adversity – and this is what had been lacking in the first half of the week.

The best scorer in the second half of the week was, in fact, Pieter-Jan Postma with a 2, 2,1, 2 scoreline, lifting him to the bronze medal position. One of the best sailors in recent years, he had never won a major championship but picked up a silver medal at the 2011 world championship and a bronze at the 2011 Olympic Test Event. He was certainly no pushover.

Høgh-Christensen and Postma had also been vilified in the British press after the race eight mark-touching incident – the Great Dane had even been marked as Public Enemy No 1 in the UK in some quarters – but the disagreement appeared to be forgotten on Friday as a cheerier Ainslie

After a week of tough racing and tough words, Jonas Høgh-Christensen and Ben Ainslie would go into the medal race on equal standing moved within the vital two points of Høgh-Christensen, effectively cancelling any points advantage. It set up a thrilling winner-takes-all scenario, providing they finished within the top seven boats.

What could be expected from the medal race? Some pundits were looking forward to an Ainslie trademark match race, but realistically that was unlikely to happen as both needed to keep half an eye on Postma. In fact, there would be two, or even three, races going on. The first would be between Høgh-Christensen and Ainslie because whoever was in front would no doubt cover the man behind pretty tightly. Everyone expected them to start close together but sail their own races until it was under control.

ATTACK OR DEFEND

Unless Postma decided to take a risk – and his style was to attack rather than defend – the second race would be for the bronze with him trying to protect his five-point lead. On the water this meant he needed to be within two places of Jonathan Lobert and Ivan Kljakovic Gaspic and within three places of Vasilij Zbogar.

Realistically, Postma could inflict damage on one of his opponents and go for the gold, but to do it to both was a tall order while also protecting his position against three other boats, all eager to fill the gap should he falter.

The third race would be for seventh place, as in the words of Rafael Trujillo, currently in 10th overall, "*No one wants to be last.*"

So what were the likely outcomes? On paper, and before the week started, the wise money would have been on Ainslie. His record in these situations was outstanding and no-one else has got close to converting tense showdowns into convincing victories. However, Høgh-Christensen had inflicted seven defeats on Ainslie out of 10 races. That was something to stop and think about. Ainslie might have turned it around in the second half of the week, but those defeats would have rubbed a sore wound in the three-time Olympic champion's mental armour.

Also, compare the indignantly angry Ainslie from Thursday against the outwardly calm and collected Høgh-Christensen. Two very different characters who thrived in different ways. Who would be more focused on the job? Who would best survive the enormous pressure that both would be under?

Ainslie didn't give much away. "*It's going to be a fascinating race; I'm really looking forward to it. It's hard to call tactics yet. It depends on the conditions and what sort of mood you are in when you get out of bed in the morning. It's going to be a very important race. It's a huge opportunity to race in front of a home crowd. Obviously there's a lot at stake, but it is going to be fantastic.*"

Høgh-Christensen was more open. "*I am not expecting too much in the medal race. PJ is only 14 points behind Ben so if we go into a full-out match race then PJ could actually go and win the Olympics. So we have to race. I hope he is set up for that as well. But you never know. That's what I hope. That would be the best for the sport and for the Olympics. We have both sailed well so far and whoever beats who is the fair winner. I've beaten him in seven races and he has beaten me in three. It's still close.*"

"*We talked before the regatta that the greatest thing would be to go into the medal race and be able to decide it yourself. And I am in that position, so I have just got to go out and sail my best. Luckily I have a good track record on the Nothe course. I won the first race and was leading the practice race, so I'll do what I can to win. I think I'll focus on my own race and knowing Ben he'll probably try something, but he can't try too much because we still have to race so PJ doesn't win. I'm really looking forward to the medal race. It will be very exciting. It will be whoever beats who, so it will be an epic battle. That is what we have here and why I love racing.*"

Assuming Høgh-Christensen and Ainslie would fight for gold and silver, there was a four way fight for the bronze. There was only so much Postma could control so most likely he was going to sail his own race and see if he got a break.

Lobert had won the silver at the 2011 Olympic Test Event; Kljakovic Gaspic had won two European Finn titles; Zbogar had already won two Olympic medals in the Laser class. All were extremely competitive sailors and with such a small points gaps between the four, nothing was certain.

Lobert put his slant on it. "*There are a lot of us close behind the first two so I'm going to have to pull out all the stops for the medal race. The medal race is different as it is shorter and the wind has a big effect. So I'll have to play the winning hand as I have nothing to lose. It will be bronze or nothing.*"

IMAGE

Whatever happened in the medal race, the conditions during the regatta had been exactly what sailing needed to improve its image. The world had finally seen sailors as athletes and perhaps finally understood the physical and technical demands of the sport. There had been strong winds, big waves, agony of sailors and pain of defeat. Viewers had watched as sailors had stretched every muscle and sinew for that extra point of speed, seen the extreme boat-handing skills required to keep the boats upright and lived the challenge of winning an Olympic medal. It had been a breath of fresh air.

So far it had all been positive news. The Finn medal race was being billed as the sailing event of the year. It was not to be missed.

SEVENTEEN
COMPELLING WEEK ENDS WITH THRILLING MEDAL RACE

Top to bottom: Ben Ainslie and Jonas Høgh-Christensen had a very close battle in the medal race • Ben Ainslie celebrating in front of the crowds • Close start with Høgh-Christensen just visible through the sails in a controlling position

AFTER WHAT HE DESCRIBED AS the hardest week of his life, Ben Ainslie took the overall lead in the regatta for the first time to take the gold medal in the London 2012 Olympic Sailing Competition. In the medal race, the leader all week, Jonas Høgh-Christensen, trailed Ainslie at every mark to lose his stranglehold on the gold. The bronze finally went to Jonathan Lobert after he dominated and won the medal race.

The whole sailing world was on the edge of its seat for 30 agonising minutes as the Finn fleet duked it out for the medals and left everyone waiting right until the thrilling ending. None of the medals were decided until the final stages of the calamitous last leg

Høgh-Christensen won the advantage over Ainslie out of the start, forcing the Brit to tack off to the right, the normally unfavoured side. The left had been favoured all week, but Ainslie through luck or judgment found a shift back to be ahead of the Dane at the top mark, though both were deep in the fleet. At the front of the fleet Ivan Kljakovic Gaspic led from Lobert.

The puffy conditions with free pumping enabled Ainslie to fly down the first run to round the gate in second behind Lobert. As the wind went lighter on the next upwind Høgh-Christensen tacked off to the right and Ainslie covered. It was nearly his undoing. The two quickly dropped to ninth and 10th on the water as the left side became favoured again.

As Lobert extended away from the fleet, on the final beat the left side came in big and Pieter-Jan Postma, the only other man who could take gold, made a spectacular recovery to round the final top mark in third. He was just one place away from taking gold as the fleet approached the final downwind mark before the short reach to the finish. Unfortunately he pushed too hard, his boom touched the back of Dan Slater's boat, and after doing his turns he was back in fifth and out of the medals.

Ainslie had stuck to Høgh-Christensen. Being so far back in the fleet, all he could do was make sure he stayed in front. He stayed there all the way to the finish to claim the gold medal to the deafening roars of the local crowd. Høgh-Christensen crossed in 10th place to take the silver, while Lobert's race win elevated him from fourth to the bronze medal. Had there ever been such a dramatic finish at the Olympics?

It had been a suspense-filled race, made even worse by the unstable puffy winds, with sailors moving up and down the fleet; the sailors kept everyone guessing to the very end. It was a made for TV thriller.

BEN AINSLIE

Ainslie said, *"It was really nerve-racking. It was a really tense race. There was a lot at stake in really difficult conditions. I was just really glad to come through it. PJ sailed really well after a great series. Jonas* as well. They both sailed so well, especially Jonas, who had one of the best series I've ever seen, so to come back was a big relief."

"The plan today was just to try and attack Jonas a bit in the start and he did a good job defending that. Then we had a split up the first beat. I'd done a bit of tuning and I thought the right was good and thankfully it worked out for me, but it was very tight."

"It's just an amazing feeling and big thanks to everyone who has supported me over the years. From being a kid down in Cornwall to my time in the Finn class I have really enjoyed every minute of it. It's fantastic."

JONAS HØGH-CHRISTENSEN

A clearly disappointed Høgh-Christensen was nevertheless upbeat about his performance. "I did what I wanted to do but it just didn't go my way. I got the start I wanted and got in the perfect position and squeezed him off the to the right. I totally followed my plan."

"Unfortunately the right paid for the first time this week. Ben put a cover on me then, probably too tight. At one point PJ had the gold."

"I am pretty happy with silver. I have lost by the smallest margin possible. Of course, that's good fun and great for the sport. But it's just a shame as I did what I wanted to do. Looking back at the week, there's a couple of races where you can gain same points, like the capsize, of course. I had the gold in my hands but just couldn't materialise it."

"It's a great achievement to win a medal. I think we've prepared really well for this Olympics and we had a pretty good game plan and followed it all week. And it's seemed to work out."

JONATHAN LOBERT

Lobert commented, "It was a crazy race and a very difficult one. I said I would do my own race and I would try to win it if I could and try not to make any mistakes and I did that. I didn't see what happened to PJ because I was already on the last reach. I heard shouting behind."

"When I started the second lap I was already in a medal position. PJ was far behind but got this magic shift on the left and came back, so I decided to make sure I won the medal race, and then this happens."

"I think this is good for the sport because we are always sailing long races so far out and, as you see, in this type of racing a lot can happen. I think it's something we should look at more for the future. It's a new game. Today for me it was good. Sometimes it's not so good but anything can happen. So I think it's much more exciting for TV."

"Jonas sailed amazingly this week. I was really surprised that he was so good. And I was also a little bit surprised that Ben was not so good. But in the end they are the two best guys on the water and I am happy to share the podium with them as I had no chance to be any better this week."

"Now I will take a small break, then I would be really pleased to join an AC team. We tried with GreenCom but that died. So I'd like to join a proper team and try something new and learn and that would be very interesting. Then slowly I will come back in the Finn for Rio."

In winning gold Ainslie became the most decorated Olympic sailor of all time. The race was watched by thousands in the sunshine on the Nothe. Thousands more were in the public access areas around it on the live beach site. And millions around the world also watched it. It probably had the largest TV audience of any sailing race in history. And if suspense and tension make good TV, then this race had it all in bucket-loads.

So, Great Britain had taken the Finn class gold medal for the fourth time running and, with ample talented sailors to take up Ainslie's mantle, perhaps this run isn't over yet.

Høgh-Christensen was the first Dane to take a Finn Olympic medal since Henning Wind in 1964, following, of course, Elvstrøm's three Finn golds

France had won the bronze again after Guillaume Florent won it in Qingdao in 2008. Lobert repeated the same feat in Weymouth by snatching it after the final race.

At the medal ceremony behind closed doors at the Weymouth & Portland Sailing Academy, the medals were presented by HRH The Princess Royal and the flowers were presented by HM King Constantine.

EIGHTEEN
MEDALISTS SPEAK OUT

SHORTLY AFTER THE END OF the Olympics the three medalists spoke about one of the toughest and closest Olympic regattas for a long time. Here are their thoughts and reflections on the regatta, their preparation, their thought processes and what the future would hold for them.

GOLD - BEN AINSLIE

HAS IT SUNK IN YET WHAT YOU HAVE ACHIEVED?
Yes and no. I was so busy after we finished racing with commitments, and then competing in the ACWS, that I never really stopped to take it all in and that's a shame in a way. Now, after some time to reflect, I am really proud of what I achieved and relieved that it was not only worthwhile for me but for all the people that gave me so much help and support.

WAS THERE ANY POINT AT WHICH YOU THOUGHT IT WASN'T GOING TO HAPPEN?
I knew after race six that something had to change if I was going to win. Jonas was on fire and I wasn't sailing that well. I was too conservative and I knew that I needed to start racing to win.

WAS DAVID GETTING WORRIED THAT YOU WEREN'T GOING TO PULL IT OFF AND WHAT WAS HE SAYING TO YOU?
Sid is probably the best coach in the world in those situations. He is completely deadpan, he doesn't change his feedback or processes he just keeps supporting you 100 per cent.

HOW DID YOU COPE WITH THE REST DAY TO COME OUT FIGHTING TO TURN IT AROUND?
The rest day probably saved me. It gave me a chance to consider what I was doing wrong, why I wasn't sailing to my best capabilities. I also took quite a lot of motivation from watching some of the other sports and Bradley Wiggins winning the cycling time trials.

HOW BADLY WAS YOUR BACK AFFECTING YOUR PERFORMANCE?
It was an issue the last six months; it had an impact on my training more than my racing; but it was just one of many issues I had to manage and deal with.

EXPLAIN THE DECISION NOT TO ANNOUNCE IT EARLIER.
To be honest, there were so many things going wrong with my body that it was just one of many issues. Everyone knew I had a problem with my back anyway so there was no point trying to make a big deal out of it. It's usually not a good idea to announce to your closest rivals that you need injections in your ankles to be able to hike, your back's knackered and you're suffering from positional vertigo.

DID A HOME GAMES LIVE UP TO EXPECTATIONS?
I think it was an amazing Games, a real credit to everyone from the organisers, the athletes to all the volunteers. Everyone in Britain was incredibly proud to have hosted such a successful event.

WOULD YOU LIKE TO SEE THE FINN REMAIN AN OLYMPIC CLASS THROUGH 2020 AND BEYOND?
I'd like to see that because I think it's still the most challenging single-hander out there for guys over 90 kg and there aren't many options in Olympic sailing for guys that big. I was initially against free pumping but I now think that the physicality it brings to the sailing is exceptional.

SUM UP THE WEEK FOR YOU.
Emotional.

SILVER - JONAS HØGH-CHRISTENSEN

HAS IT SUNK IN YET WHAT YOU HAVE ACHIEVED?
There is no doubt that the achievement in winning the silver was fantastic and I am very happy with the result in all. But when that is said, it will haunt me forever that I did not win. Nobody thought Ben could be beaten, but I knew that if I sailed my very best I could do it. I made one too many mistakes during the qualifying races that ended up costing vital points before the medal race.

HOW DO YOU NOW FEEL ABOUT WINNING THE SILVER MEDAL?
I feel good. Very good. But again it still haunts me that I did not win. I was too close to winning for it not to leave a mental scar. I am still not able to watch the medal race and probably never will be.

HAVING DOMINATED THE FIRST HALF OF THE WEEK, WAS IT HARD TO MENTALLY COPE WITH A DAY OFF?
A bit. I was feeling good going into that day off and felt that I was dominating. We knew and had prepared for the last two days being much harder than the first three. The reason being that we would sail on the south race course that would favour Ben a lot. We had 50 metres a minute of current going against the wind. That meant the beats were shorter and the downwinds were very long. That would play into Ben's strong sides and my weak sides. On top of that I had some unpleasant experiences with vandalism of my car. Great Britain did not show its greatest colours at that moment, but in all I found a lot of support, respect and compassion from the British supporters.

HOW STRONG WAS YOUR BELIEF THAT YOU COULD WIN THE GOLD ON THE MORNING OF THE MEDAL RACE?
I had no doubt that I could win. I had a clear plan. We knew that Ben would probably try and rattle me by trying to match race me. I had

measured the time it would take to get to the place on the line where I wanted to start. The plan was to let Ben follow me in so he would start to windward of me. The reason was that during our extensive training and during the first race the left side of the course was clearly favoured. The plan went totally as planned. Ben came and I used the committee boat to keep him at bay while staying right of the start line.

At 40 seconds I knew I had to bail and go for the line. I had Ben where I wanted him and soon after the start I could squeeze him off to the right. But sailing has always been a game of chances, especially on the Nothe course, and this time it did not go my way. I don't blame the course, but if I had been 4-8 points further ahead it would have been a totally different game and my chances would have been much better.

WHAT HAS BEEN THE REACTION BACK HOME TO THE MEDAL AND HAS IT OPENED NEW OPPORTUNITIES?
The reaction has been amazing. People have been great and sailing has been the talk of the Olympics. About 1.2 million people watched the medal race in a 6 million people nation. That is the same rating as when our national football team plays a world's qualifier. I have been offered many TV shows but turned them down.

I hope that this experience will open up more sailing opportunities for the nation. I would like to create both a Danish Volvo team and an AC45 team. If we could promote sailing from Optis and all the way to the seniors, whether it be racing or cruising, that would be fantastic.

WHAT ARE YOU GOING TO DO NEXT IN TERMS OF ANY SAILING PLANS?
Right now I have officially no plans. I would like to be involved in larger teams and I am sure I have a lot to offer a team. What the future brings nobody knows. I am fortunate to have a 'real' job, so sailing is not life or death to me. That makes it so much more enjoyable actually.

IS THERE ANYTHING YOU'D DO DIFFERENTLY, GIVEN THE CHANCE TO DO IT ALL AGAIN?
Not really. This time around I got to do it my way. Looking back at a 12-month comeback I think I did great. I finished fourth and third at the 2011 and 2012 Worlds. I got that Olympic medal that I aimed for, even though it wasn't the colour that I aimed for. I managed to give the 'best' sailor of our time a run for his money and ended up at the top of the recently announced World Ranking. All in all it is hard to find anything that needed to be changed.

WOULD YOU LIKE TO SEE THE FINN REMAIN AN OLYMPIC CLASS THROUGH 2020 AND BEYOND?
Honestly, some years ago I thought that the Finn was slowly going out of fashion. But the changes to the class rules have made it the most

interesting and toughest class at the Olympics. No class demands more fitness, tactical racing and technical work. The battles are always close and the sailors are colourful. I am sure that if you did research into what class had more viewers and news coverage, the Finn would win by a mile.

SUM UP THE WEEK FOR YOU.
The most exhilarating week of my life.

BRONZE - JONATHAN LOBERT

WHAT ARE YOUR REFLECTIONS ON WINNING A MEDAL, ESPECIALLY AFTER SUCH A DRAMATIC MEDAL RACE?
As I said all week, I knew that the Games would be a very tight competition. I knew that I won't be the fastest upwind but for sure really good on the runs. I just tried to never give up on any boat I could catch and try to focus on myself. In the medal race I knew I couldn't control all the guys so I just sailed my race. After all, you can always say I could have done better, but I am really happy with the bronze.

WHAT HAS BEEN THE REACTION BACK HOME TO THE MEDAL?
People were very nice to me. A lot of non-sailors told me that they saw the end of the medal race live on the French TV. It is really nice to see the eyes of the kids when they see the medal. I try to put Olympic sailing under the lights and try to make the people realise that it is a great sport.

YOU WERE VERY POSITIVE ALL WEEK. WHAT WAS THE PLAN GOING INTO THE MEDAL RACE?
As I told you I love the medal race. It's short and always very intense. You have to be full-on all the time. My plan going on the water was simply get some clear air, sail fast and give all you can to have no regrets.

SUM UP THE RACING OVER THE WHOLE WEEK FOR THE WHOLE FLEET?
I think in the Finn we had a very consistent week as the top guys didn't make any big scores. I thought I would sail all week with Vasilij and Bambi, and it was always a big fight between us. Jonas had something more upwind and Ben was always around. I really enjoyed the weather and the waves.

HAS THE MEDAL WIN OPENED NEW OPPORTUNITIES FOR YOU?
For now nothing, but I hope to get some new sponsors to be able to not lose money on the next campaign. I would like to join the America's Cup and try some big boat regattas, so I am open to any solicitations.

DID THE OLYMPICS LIVE UP TO YOUR EXPECTATIONS?
Yes. It is really a different regatta but it is so good to be part of it.

WHAT ARE YOU GOING TO DO NEXT IN TERMS OF ANY SAILING PLANS?
For now I take a break with my Finn, but I will back next year in Palma to start a new campaign. For the rest everything is still open.

WOULD YOU LIKE TO SEE THE FINN REMAIN AN OLYMPIC CLASS THROUGH 2020 AND BEYOND AND WHY?
Of course the Finn needs to stay in the Games. It is the last boat for the big guys. It's also very good-looking on TV, especially with the free pumping with the onboard camera. I think we need, as the class, to try to make to something more attractive to the public. The medal race format is great – it's intense, close to shore and a lot can happen. I think we need more races like the first one in the Games to have the public taking part. We need to mix a bit of the classic sailing race and this new format. Like that the Finn will be, as before, an experimental boat going forward.

SUM UP THE WEEK FOR YOU.
A lot of emotions, stress and pain but so much fun.

NINETEEN
AS ONE ERA ENDS
A NEW ONE BEGINS

While some sailors moved on from the class after the 2012 Olympic Games, some were already preparing for the challenge of Rio 2016.

THE CLOSING OF THE LONDON 2012 Olympic Sailing Competition was also perhaps the end of a magnificent era within the Finn class. With three-time Finn gold medalist Ben Ainslie announcing that he was very unlikely to ever set foot in a Finn again, his decade of domination was complete and he left the stage open for a new generation of heroes to take his place.

The goodbyes were not just limited to Ainslie. Almost a dozen of those who competed at Weymouth and Portland had probably sailed their final Finn regatta and hung up their hiking pants one last time. The game is changing at a fast pace. The new generation are younger, taller, stronger and fitter than ever before. And they are all hungry for success.

Silver medalist Jonas Høgh-Christensen pointed this just before the Games, *"I love the Finn and think it has gotten a revival with the new physical aspects. It is for sure the hardest boat on the Olympic programme. Real athletes pushing super-hard. Next time around there will be no old school sailors with a bit too much fat. They will be fit, tall and young. With that said, it looks like my time is up."*

ELITE

The group of elite athletes that was the Finn fleet at London 2012 had trained together, competed against each other and enjoyed the thrill of the battle together for most of their adult life. Many had done two or three Olympics. Some were newcomers, but all had faced the journey together, living the old cliché, 'The journey is the reward.'

As we witnessed during the competition, the sailors could be ruthless on the water but had a great sense of camaraderie off the water. Bronze medalist Jonathan Lobert put it best, *"The most important thing I learned in the Finn class is that it is possible to sail like gentlemen – enemies on the water, but very good friends on the shore."*

While the older sailors had perhaps had their day in the limelight, the young are ready to move in to try and emulate their heroes. Many of those sailing in London 2012, and some who missed selection, have already started their campaign for Rio 2016. But there was no easy route. It will be a long hard road of perseverance and dedication. Some of those who learned valuable lessons in 2012 will be those who will shine in 2016. London 2012 is behind us and we look forward to the challenges that Rio 2016 will bring.

HIGHLIGHT

The battle in the Finn class proved to be the highlight of the sailing competition at London 2012. Quite how it played out no-one could have guessed, but it turned into a nail-biter right through to the closing minutes of the very last race.

The best sailor of the opening series was undoubtedly Høgh-Christensen. The best sailor in the medal race was probably Lobert. Meanwhile, Ainslie was making headlines because he was not producing the dominating performance that everyone expected. He said, "*It is always hard when people say you are a dead cert to win; you try to tell them that is not the case, but they don't listen.*"

Though Høgh-Christensen ran away with the first half of the competition in terms of a points lead, in fairness, Ainslie had also put together a pretty good series. His only problem was that the Dane had beaten him in all six races.

PRESSURE

Then, in the second half of the week, Høgh-Christensen started making a few mistakes. He'd already had a start boat collision in race four and then a capsize in race seven perhaps showed the pressure was getting to him. Ainslie did what he does best. He pounced, grabbed the opportunity by the throat and sank his teeth in hard so he couldn't let go. With a grimace of determination on his face, he gradually clawed back the points gap going into the deciding medal race.

In spite of that comeback, however, Ainslie was clearly under par, we later learned in pain, and in the end, probably quite lucky to come away with the gold. While he struggled with making comebacks in most races, Høgh-Christensen was making them with much more regularity, his epic speed taking him to the front for a while in all but a few races. Only once or twice did Ainslie show the kind of form that had made him the out-and-out pre-regatta favourite for the gold.

MINEFIELD

The Nothe spectator area provided a great view of the minefield of windshifts and holes on the medal race course, right across to the Portland Harbour wall on the far side. It played havoc within the fleet. We were told it was a price everyone had to pay, though some paid more dearly than others. In the medal race, for the first time the whole week, the right paid on the first beat, which negated the advantage Høgh-Christensen had over Ainslie out of the start.

From then on it became a simple match race between the two best-performing sailors of the week. Ainslie led Høgh-Christensen at the top mark and once he had control he never let it go. There was a heart-stopping moment when Pieter-Jan Postma emerged from a big left shift on the final beat to round the final top mark in third on a last minute charge. One more place for Postma and the gold would have been heading to The Netherlands – but it wasn't to be.

You have to feel sorry for Postma. He had done enough for a medal but for some reason decided to push for the gold, rather than consolidate

for silver or bronze. In many ways it was a brave move, but one that ultimately left him without a medal of any colour. It was barely 50 metres to the finish and he had a medal in his hands. As he tried to pass Dan Slater, the end of his boom touched the back of Slater's boat.

Slater explained, *"I said to him, 'Mate you've got a medal. Don't have a go here. It's not on.' I was in a good position to beat Rafa for seventh overall so I had a race on myself. I felt for PJ because he totally made a meal of it. But that's the pressure of these things. He had a medal sewn up and he took a big risk considering where we were and the timing of it."*

In the end Høgh-Christensen's mistakes, combined with Postma's rash move in the medal race, all conspired to hand the gold medal to Ainslie. It seemed like he was destined to win it all along, to irrefutably make his mark in sailing history.

NEXT GENERATION

With both Ainslie and Høgh-Christensen hinting at their 'retirement' from the class – Ainslie stated, *"It can never get any better than this and I'm not sure I would want to go through it again,"* while Høgh-Christensen said, *"I don't have any sights for Rio. I've been talking with Ben about this and we'd either like to see it on TV or go there as commentators"* – what of the next generation?

Bronze medalist Lobert is typical of the kind of sailor the class is now attracting. He towers over most of his fellow sailors, is many years younger and is at the peak of his career. He is the epitome of the new-generation Finn sailor: very tall, very fit, very strong and very athletic. Just watch him move around the boat and you'll understand.

Some are saying the Finn medal race was probably the most watched race in Olympic sailing history. About 70,000 people are thought to have descended on Weymouth to watch Ainslie secure his fourth gold medal and overcome the Great Dane. The spectator area was full to capacity. The free areas on either side were straining at the seams, while more than 3,000 had gathered on the stone pier. Thousands more filled the free live site on Weymouth Beach.

SPECTATORS

There is no doubt that having spectators at the sailing events proved very popular with the spectators, while the sailors clearly loved it and thrived on the atmosphere it created. For some, the cheering crowd was the high point of the week, while others would have preferred a fairer playing field instead of a show in front of the public.

In how many other Olympic sports have the requirements of the spectators, and the TV audience, been allowed to take precedence over the quality of racing? It may have been the same for everyone, but elements of randomness and luck were always present.

And so, after 10 years of Ainslie domination, it certainly does seem like the end of an era. Ainslie left the door slightly open with a 'never say never' comment; but he also dropped enough hints that this would be the last time we see him in a Finn, and maybe the last time at the Olympics. After a decade at the top he has not only broken all the records in the class but made new ones that are unlikely ever to be broken. Along the way he achieved the highest accolade the Finn class can bestow on its sailors with his entry into the Hall of Fame way back in 2004. Since then he has won three more world titles and two more Olympic gold medals. It was quite a run.

ERA

If we have written the last chapter of the Ainslie era in the Finn class then it has been a privilege to watch. Almost single-handedly he took Finn sailing to a whole new level of excellence and focused the spotlight of the world's media on the toughest Olympic class of them all.

But the class is already moving on. As one era ends, a new one is about to begin.

FINAL RESULTS
LONDON 2012 OLYMPIC SAILING COMPETITION
FINN CLASS

Pos	NOC	Crew	1	2	3	4	5	6	7	8	9	10	MR	Total	Net
1	GBR	Ben Ainslie	2	2	6	(12)	4	3	1	3	6	1	18	58	46
2	DEN	Jonas Høgh-Christensen	1	1	2	7	1	2	(8)	4	5	3	20	54	46
3	FRA	Jonathan Lobert	9	4	4	2	6	7	5	(10)	3	7	2	59	49
4	NED	Pieter-Jan Postma	5	10	3	4	(20)	13	2	2	1	2	10	72	52
5	CRO	Ivan Kljakovic Gaspic	3	3	7	9	5	6	3	7	4	(10)	8	65	55
6	SLO	Vasilij Zbogar	8	6	5	3	8	5	(9)	6	2	6	14	72	63
7	NZL	Dan Slater	7	11	1	6	(17)	11	6	15	8	14	4	100	83
8	ESP	Rafael Trujillo Villar	12	12	12	(23)	7	4	15	1	13	4	6	109	86
9	SWE	Daniel Birgmark	(17)	5	14	1	9	9	10	12	10	8	12	107	90
10	FIN	Tapio Nirkko	11	13	8	5	3	12	4	5	15	(17)	16	109	92
11	EST	Deniss Karpak	(14)	9	11	11	11	1	7	13	11	11		99	85
12	USA	Zach Railey	10	15	13	17	2	8	12	8	12	(19)		116	97
13	AUS	Brendan Casey	dnf	7	dpi	14	10	17	19	9	9	5		131	106
14	GRE	Ioannis Mitakis	4	21	10	8	ocs	10	20	19	7	9		133	108
15	CAN	Gregory Douglas	16	(23)	16	13	12	18	13	17	20	12		160	137
16	POL	Piotr Kula	dsq	16	17	16	13	20	ocs	11	14	16		173	148
17	RUS	Eduard Skornyakov	13	8	(22)	15	19	22	16	16	22	22		175	153
18	TUR	Alican Kaynar	18	14	18	18	dne	14	11	(22)	16	20		176	154
19	UKR	Olexsiy Borysov	rdg	rdg	19	19	15	19	(23)	14	17	18		183.6	160.6
20	BRA	Jorge João Zarif	15	20	15	20	16	(24)	14	21	19	21		185	161
21	CZE	Michael Maier	19	18	21	10	18	(23)	18	20	23	15		185	162
22	ITA	Filippo Baldassari	20	22	(24)	21	14	21	17	18	18	13		188	164
23	AUT	Florian Raudaschl	6	19	23	24	ocs	15	21	24	24	23		204	179
24	CHN	Lei Gong	ocs	17	20	22	ocs	16	22	23	21	24		215	190

© IOC. Official results powered by ATOS Origin. Timing and results management by Omega.

OLYMPIC MEDALISTS 1952-2012

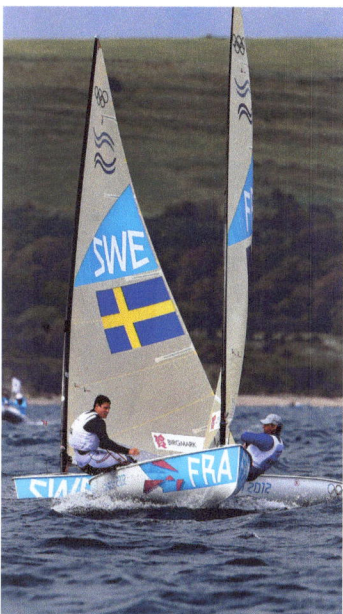

1952, HELSINKI, FINLAND
1 Paul Elvstrøm, Denmark
2 Charles Currey, Great Britain
3 Rickard Sarby, Sweden

1956, MELBOURNE, AUSTRALIA
1 Paul Elvstrøm, Denmark
2 André Nelis, Belgium
3 John Marvin, USA

1960, NAPLES, ITALY
1 Paul Elvstrøm, Denmark
2 Alexander Chuchelov, USSR
3 André Nelis, Belgium

1964, ENOSHIMA, JAPAN
1 Willy Kuhweide, Germany
2 Peter Barrett, USA
3 Henning Wind, Denmark

1968, ACAPULCO, MEXICO
1 Valentin Mankin, USSR
2 Hubert Raudaschl, Austria
3 Fabio Albarelli, Italy

1972, KIEL, WEST GERMANY
1 Serge Maury, France
2 Elias Hatzipavlis, Greece
3 Victor Potapov, USSR

1976, KINGSTON, CANADA
1 Jochen Schümann, DDR
2 Andrei Balashov, USSR
3 John Bertrand, Australia

1980, TALLINN, USSR
1 Esko Rechardt, Finland
2 Wolfgang Mayrhofer, Austria
3 Andrei Balashov, USSR

1984, LONG BEACH, USA
1 Russell Coutts, New Zealand
2 John Bertrand, USA
3 Terry Neilson, Canada

1988, PUSAN, KOREA
1 José Luis Doreste, Spain
2 Peter Holmberg, US Virgin Islands
3 John Cutler, New Zealand

1992, BARCELONA, SPAIN
1 José Maria van der Ploeg, Spain
2 Brian Ledbetter, USA
3 Craig Monk, New Zealand

1996, SAVANNAH, USA
1 Mateusz Kusznierewicz, Poland
2 Sebastien Godefroid, Belgium
3 Roy Heiner, The Netherlands

2000, SYDNEY, AUSTRALIA
1 Iain Percy, Great Britain
2 Luca Devoti, Italy
3 Fredrik Lööf, Sweden

2004, ATHENS, GREECE
1 Ben Ainslie, Great Britain
2 Rafael Trujillo, Spain
3 Mateusz Kusznierewicz, Poland

2008, QINGDAO, CHINA
1 Ben Ainslie, Great Britain
2 Zach Railey, USA
3 Guillaume Florent, France

2012, WEYMOUTH & PORTLAND, UK
1 Ben Ainslie, Great Britain
2 Jonas Høgh-Christensen, Denmark
3 Jonathan Lobert, France

ACKNOWLEDGEMENTS

The author would like to thank all those sailors who responded to interviews and questions before, during and after the 2012 Olympic Games. Without this valuable and much appreciated assistance – at a time when you are highly focused and resistant to distractions – these reports would not have been possible.

Thanks, also, to François Richard for most of the excellent photos within this book. All photos are by François except pp8-11 (IFA Archive), and cover, pp12-22, pp25-36, p50 (top), p54 (top), p58 (top), p59 and p64 which are by Robert Deaves/Finn Class.

www.ingramcontent.com/pod-product-compliance
Lightning Source LLC
Chambersburg PA
CBHW042017080426
42735CB00002B/78